I0583804

NEO-DECADENCE: 12 MANIFESTOS

EDITED BY
JUSTIN ISIS

THIS IS A SNUGGLY BOOK

ISBN: 978-1-64525-063-0

The cover shows a detail from: *The Color Run, Grand Prix Edition (Melbourne 2014)*, by Chris Phutully.
https://creativecommons.org/licenses/by/2.0/deed.en

CONTENTS

NEO-DECADENCE: 12 MANIFESTOS

NEO-DECADENCE (I)

Brendan Connell

1. Words are only words, a somewhat artificial simulation of nature, and should not be given too much importance. Slick writing should be tossed out like men with sweaty hands, mass-produced objects, and food in Styrofoam cups.

2. Never imitate yourself. The writing should be artificial and shallow, without contrived emotions. Then maybe something will be realised. There is already enough sadness in life. Soak the book in gasoline if it must be soaked in something.

3. Character development is synthetic. It should be resorted to only with a certain amount of shame.

4. If it be political let it lurch to the left, burrow underground so that tall buildings tumble off their hinges.

5. Story arcs should only be used to hang oneself with. Nothing is ever resolved. Nothing progresses.

6. Syntax should be dredged out of old books, trimmed off of far-away planets, stripped from dreams. Trivial things should be said in a grandiose manner meant to disgust collegiate scribblers and make the lips of pseudo-great novelists twist in anger.

7. Kublai Khan was a modern. Things fell apart a long time ago. We are already living in the ruins of civilisation. There's nothing to celebrate. When you toast, make sure you smash your glasses together. This kind of writing should be the same. Harmony is overrated.

8. Forget about the sound of cars, missiles, clever machines and originality, since nothing is less original. There are enough monsters and demons in the real world without needing to look elsewhere.

9. Great developments don't come about by listlessly trying to please the crowd. They'll forget in a minute. If the only thing left is a fragment, it better be good. If you're lucky, you'll end up like some choliambic poet.

10. There's nothing wrong with writing a lousy book. Just make sure it's really lousy. There is nothing worse than competence.

11. Neo-Decadent writers will honour the fragmented, the contorted, the unfinished, the unpublished. Realising there is no glory, no reward, no lavish suppers or dancing on tables. Living in obscure lanes and remote canyons,

things will be written in unread languages or translated from the language of lizards and snakes, plagiarised from deep wells and signed with hands wet with the dew of rotting fruit.

12. Nothing comes to an end. Let a little light shine through the darkness and remember that when the universe collapses in on itself you can read the novel back to front.

NEO-DECADENCE (II)

Justin Isis

1. A goat wanders at random, putting things in its mouth.

2. NO SUSTAINABILITY.

3. The kidneys are the prime organ of Neo-Decadence. The pink Gemini. Filtering. Most educated people have equally educated kidneys, which means they try to tell stories instead of pissing when needed. Keep an eye out for these creatures and their awards.

4. No precedence is given to the Decadent writers of the 19th century, their modes or milieu. Neo-Decadence is more likely to cross 1990s video game dialogue with the structure of a 16th century picaresque to discuss a drug deal in present day Mongolia. Fealty and earnestness can only hold back progress. We do not have saints, and we consume our idols.

5. Literature is not a guild system. Academies and work-shops: a parade of inbred dogs with each generation more unfit than the last.

6. Writing can be neither sincere nor authentic; these are the cliches of the ranks of the dead. Style is a mute scream in symbols—that's all.

7. There is nothing to learn, but much to steal.

WOMEN'S FASHION

Justin Isis

1. Gold.

2. Symmetry remains the enemy; lopsided designs must proliferate. Shoes must be dialogues rather than chiral clones. The flapping of a lone, broken wing. Heterochromia as guiding principle.

3. Black and white will be replaced with approximations: ivory and seashell, midnight blue and café noir, cream and suet, flax, bone, champagne and charcoal, phthalocyanine green. Monotones, long the refuge of the unimaginative, must be banished.

4. All progress begins with cultural appropriation, but the ligaments and tendons must be severed. We take pleasure in the displacement and defamiliarization of ancestral costumes, including suits, skirts and hats of all sorts. "Quality" materials will be replaced with cheap synthetics, while modern streetwear will take on a ceremonial aspect, newly replete with hand-stitched

additions and emendations: markers of mood, the badges of imaginary offices. The Neo-Decadent Woman is post-nationalist and Post-Naturalist, proudly suturing together the haute and the gothic, the sleekly functional and the lumberingly decorative. Endlessly repurposing found materials, she drapes herself in garments patched with the logos of defunct brands, strung with skeins of dandelions and trailing assorted scraps and rags.

5. Simplicity is the enemy of beauty, since fundamentally stupid and regressive types will always revert to minimalism, little realizing that even a nude figure itself is nothing but a mass of visual artifices, and the human body an additive assemblage with its useless adjuncts and vestigial blind alleys, steeped in archaism and ceaselessly recapitulating obsolete pomp. A woman with her wisdom teeth and appendix intact has no need to scoff at frameless glasses or a bathing suit concealed beneath another bathing suit, much less a mask of bone or a live plant for a necklace.

6. The parade model of fashion with its hermetic collections watered down for commercial retail has led to intolerable stagnation. The runway must be abolished, reintegrated into everyday life.

7. Rather than transforming every woman into a walking synthesis of the universe, contemporary "fast fashion" has isolated them in conformity. In response, the Neo-Decadent Woman aspires to the confrontational and extravagant rather than the merely pretty and propor-

tional, altering and improvising her wardrobe when necessary, restoring hygiene and civility. Vulgar sleeves may be slashed off and new ornaments stitched on, while two bland shirts may be torn apart and combined. Vintage items must be similarly altered, lest any fraudulent glamor adhere to the unmodified past. Garments must be modular and progressive, with each season's designs giving birth to the next: fresh evolutions, lineages caught in flux.

8. To the uninformed and outdated, the Neo-Decadent Woman manifests as a parody of their naive notions of taste. If she appears at times as a jarring burlesque, it is only because she aims to exceed whatever merely practical conventions burden the rest of the populace, while ignoring the naive fancies of would-be suitors and designers seeking to reduce her to a prop for their own vanity. Tedious ghosts of "good taste" haunt our cities, and they must be immediately and boldly exorcized. If passéists react with disgust or bewilderment, let them confine themselves to their rooms: the streets will not miss them.

9. Contemporary electronic couture must function as a constant typographic-pictorial provocation, integrating all manner of VR and AR accoutrements in service of its wearer's psychic image-repertoire. LED skirts, photo-sensitive cosmetics, telehaptic fabrics and smart textiles with distributed audio systems will turn women heading out for a night on the town into noisy and irradiated apparitions, glorious nocturnal butterflies congregating

in city centres, the folds of their dresses stirred by volup-tuous vibrations and suffused with clouds of informa-tion, every available surface alive with images and words while remotely transmitting sensations to wearers of compatible clothing—receptive friends and prospective lovers: the chattering of outfits, a promiscuous public psychokinesis.

A. Vinyl boots.
B. Hats that absorb moonlight.
C. Nylon spiderweb veils.

Crowds of women should be seen and heard from a great distance, riots of convulsive colour and sound updating themselves in real time. Social media's tendency towards curated extroversion must assume its ultimate form, extending onto the body and displaying itself to each woman's advantage. Constantly inflicting herself on the urban environment, the Neo-Decadent Woman sifts and strains ambient signals like an aquatic filter feeder, immersed in the currents of communal space: the prime and beautiful anti-neutral proponent of a truly unitary MODE.

10. The Neo-Decadent Woman as beekeeper: discrete pieces of information engulf her, forming transitory veils and wreaths of rumour, insect-perfect algorithms swarming across her limbs like the friendly furry buzzing of small warm bodies.

11. Fashion will now consciously express every sort of human relationship. Careful adherence to truly precise and accurate correspondences has until now been rare, but to neglect what one's contemporaries are wearing can no longer be permitted. The Neo-Decadent Woman with countless friends and lovers attires herself different-ly when in proximity to each of them, presenting diverse accents and aspects, not as reactive supplication, but as direct, balanced commentary. To restore human compas-sion demands total attentiveness; an almost Confucian fidelity underlies what on the surface appear to be ran-dom decisions and arbitrary bricolage. How could it be permissible for an architect to attire herself in the same manner as an athlete? Should a woman setting out to meet a long-lost friend consider herself blameless when the conjunction of their outfits in a photograph presents an offensive mismatch? A bland equality has been driz-zled over the streets like syrup, resulting in widespread, self-absorbed paralysis; everywhere strangers dress alike regardless of their station, while indifferent lovers amble through an evening's entertainment like clashing instru-ments failing to achieve harmony, the spiritual essences of their clothes recoiling from each other even as their lips and hands touch. Coordinated outfits are the correct counter to these absurdities, their colours and designs enacting a subtle cabalism.

12. Time and space died a long time ago, leaving behind fossilized remains ripe for excavation and creative re-assembly. Fashion strata of the past must yield fanciful chimeras, with entire time periods sampled in light of

each other, suggesting new relationships appropriate to our novel sensibilities (if necessary, grist garments may be renamed, the better to remove their tired cultural baggage. Clothes, like words, are filthy with associative detritus: to reinstate spontaneity demands some surgical measure of sartorial neologism). The outline of an Edwardian golfing costume may find itself accented with a head scarf and assorted plastic raver accessories, while a bridal train heavy with beads may be repurposed for use on the subway. Kimono-hijab hybrids in bright primary colours may be printed with the texts of entire poems and stories. A humble soutane, recoloured a poisonous cobalt yellow and ornamented with metallic spikes and pauldrons, would present appropriate morning wear for a young woman heading to work, suggesting a faithful, predatory centipede lured by the light of the sun rising through polluted clouds; the evocations of youthful vigour, plasmic haze and indescribably beautiful envenomed fangs would all create a unified impression in the mind of an admiring observer.

13. Conventional significations of femininity must be taken as mere stylistic tendencies rather than elaborations upon an essential nature or confirmations of commodified social roles. We extol the femininity of a general's uniform, retooled and recoloured, its medals melted or melded into a corsage of metal, suggesting a willowy military of the streets, all glowing athletic violence. A young mother with a child strapped to her back becomes a Janus, and must attire herself and the infant

in matching costumes: perhaps masks of Tragedy and Comedy, or the silhouettes of Isis and Horus: better yet, faceless larval gods, figures not yet imagined.

14. Notions of age progression and "appropriateness" must be abolished: older women, still vital, must not take on drab and restrained tones, while younger women should avoid slipping into the "elegant" lassitude of clichéd "classics," relying on mere youth to stand in for real style. Each year of a woman's life presents nearly limitless entry points into expressive potential.

15. Elderly women may impudently don tiaras at any time.

16. It is safe to say that almost no human civilization has perfected the role of gloves, which are so central to the current moment as to be indisputable. Women's gloves must be taken as seriously as battle campaigns, since by sampling the atmosphere of a location or gathering, their role is identical to that of advance scouts capable of any necessary infiltration.

17. Hats should be monuments to impertinent aggression, aristocratic extrusions of a violent hunger for fresh experience. Better a pschent or conical crown than a beret or bonnet.

18. Neo-Decadent sportswomen require appropriate outfits even when not engaged in their physical pursuits of choice. We imagine their activities trailing after them in their free hours, their achievements of the past and

goals of the future present as physical shadows extending into three dimensions: topologies, lines of force. Moreso even than the clothing of painters or surgeons, their leisurewear must have its own domestic economy, reaching into geometric realms for inspiration: angular hems, fractal schemes, prominently toroidal dresses.

19. Purses, handbags and wallets require in truth their own manifesto, but it is enough to stress that their designs must be consonant with the principles established thus far, and that advances in 3D printing mean the pace of their evolution will only increase. If possible, they should be replaced rapidly and viewed as the equivalent of ephemeral whims, containers of stray thoughts as much as vital objects.

20. Denim must be regarded as the equivalent of a particularly troublesome and piquant spice, resorted to rarely. It is not intended for daily wear, and its overuse has done much to cheapen and degrade our culture.

21. A triangular umbrella is correct.

22. Specifically erotic costumes must be elaborate in the extreme, reclaiming the heritage of the priestess and the courtesan: their preparation should take hours if not days, involving multiple layers to be unwrapped, unfolded and untied, with as many hidden colours as sea creatures and all manner of diverse textures and strange perfumes. The Neo-Decadent Woman may arrive at an assignation wearing sex armour and a sex helmet,

propped up on towering platforms and vibrating with her own internal energy like an astronaut visitor from a planet of refined desire. Her clothes will provide their own soundtrack, the pitch elevating with the removal of each layer, the folds of her garments adorned with lascivious sigils and symbols, their surfaces streaming records of previous encounters intended to entice her lover into an erotic loop, past pleasures recaptured in the present embrace: or else bare mirror surfaces reflecting their inevitable narcissism, allowing them to behold themselves as they approach. The innermost layers must be diaphanous, dissolving at the touch.

23. Crustaceans cannot grow in a linear fashion like most other animals, yet some are significantly invasive. Similarly, the woman who takes pains to dress for a picnic in a desert of burning plastic feels no disappointment when confronted with a horizon of violets extending to infinity.

24. Human cylinders of shining introspection.

25. Plastic violet infinity.

MEN'S FASHION

Gaurav Monga
Justin Isis

1. Men's fashion has always congratulated itself for its unoriginality, and to read most descriptions of it is to gag on supposed superlatives that stick in one's mouth like stones: sober, sombre, serious, dependable, durable. These are qualities we would prize in an undertaker, but not in the kind of man we would like to install in any capacity of our everyday lives, much less value for his appearance. We, the Neo-Decadents, with no certainty of the future and no attachment to the world as it stands, naturally have little sympathy for the garments with which the industrial world of the past few centuries has expected us to conceal ourselves. The lauded tailors of the past: over-rewarded pruners of cobwebs.

2. All business attire is abrogate, null and void, historical effluvia. We would define ourselves as gentlemen except that, subsisting in leisure, there is little about us to warrant the term. Gentility in the modern sense belongs to the professionals, those virtuous beasts of burden: leisure

23

is cultivated savagery. Autocratic predators of sensation, our clothing must be more pitilessly stylized than the world has until now allowed, in the manner of handsome wasps lazily hovering, venomous, variegated.

3. The exaggerated reverence for 'reputable' designers and 'high end' brands must first be adulterated like cheap wine, then pissed away as easily. The fashion weeks of Tokyo, London, Paris and New York have come to embody all the silly solemnity of church services. Luxury brand outlets—shrines to insipidly 'tasteful' merchandise, presided over by sales assistants as nauseating as any effete cleric—should be profaned and robbed whenever possible. Stolen items should be treated carelessly and altered, or simply given to children to do with as they please.

4. We renounce all passéist productions of fast fashion brands, which merely jacket and sleeve men as if laminating them in hasty terror. Our musical subcultures with their sew-on patches and badges betray an ardent and seemly hunger for heraldry, and in response we will reinstate emblems, crests and coats-of-arms. These will refer to our own moods and ambitions rather than the mere continuity of our blood: sigil-suits, external records of visions. This will demand a new blazon language:

Splenetic green, sarcasm counterchanged
Homeless Petronius
Unaffianced artist-arbiter of graffiti
Hooded rags, thereon

An X engrailed
Crazed and discerning in fresh aerosols
Holographic tags, drone eyes rampant
Slashed sleeves
Mercury Junior, regret untenanted
Secret owner
Of Barcelona

5. We welcome all synthetic fabrics and up-to-date elements of electronic couture: the concept of "quality"
materials is an unlovely anachronism. We prize daring
and originality over laborious production, and we disdain overpriced and exploitative rubbish, false scarcity
and inflated prestige. Both the dismal and outdated costumes of tailors and the valueless stunt concoctions of
runway-focused designers are to be replaced with recombinant and modular garments distributed in a decentral-
ized fashion. As the mundane and regular pose death
to innovation, the Neo-Decadent Man should inspire
in others clothes that smack of the extreme: polar ends,
furry frontier hoods, clothes that not so much announce
a mission to obscure destinations or outer spheres but
carry us to the ends of the Earth.

6. Mills will soon shut down, mills that once produced
superfluous denim in outpost remains of erstwhile em-
pires. There will be no looms, no weavers singing songs
while stitching intricate embroidery on outmoded
shawls; nor will anyone lament the demise of the mills,
the looms or the weavers. We will celebrate clothes con-
stituted so differently that an entirely alien and novel

function of attire will emerge: clothing of the spirit, and the spirit will not sympathize with the weakness of a bygone era. There will be nothing that smacks of Nature in these clothes—except to the extent that Nature has always secretly desired plastics, nylons and printable electronics, and the mineral kingdom has always relied on us to keep it current. We must do our best to furnish the chemical elements with fresh configurations for our coordinated outfits.

7. AR clothing will extend an outfit's dimensions to the surrounding environment, eliminating the distinction between public and personal space; we will soon wear clothes that possess colour and volume but are essentially fabricless, bearing no cloth. A group of Neo-Decadent Men will produce their own atmosphere, becoming literal advertisements for themselves, the patterns of their robes spreading to nearby information surfaces, their moods visible. The Neo-Decadent Man's shadow will be treated as another accessory, a portal to his past displaying media extensions, personal profiles, recent thoughts and improvised images.

8. The Neo-Decadent Man will finally free himself from the dull, dreary, and melancholic. He will cease to read novels situated in tiny Nordic pastoral landscapes and will dress boldly, without any fear. He will cease to wear cardigans or any other depressing garment associated with grey days and nostalgia for childhood. The material of his clothes will be unlike any corduroy or similar material that gathers dust, fabric that refuses to remember;

instead, it will equip him with vestments that show that he has overcome the failures and impediments of his past.

9. We have nothing but contempt for the quaint revivalist who favours the fancy dress of the 18th or 19th century, including all spiritual descendants of that syphilitic dullard Beau Brummell. Similarly, we have no concern with masculinity defined as the mere absence of conventionally feminine traits—neither in the regressive sense of affirming it, nor in the naively reactionary sense of protesting it. Rather than macerate male style in a welter of agonized self-contradiction, we prize stylistic experiments incorporating the expansion of its true sentiments and tendencies: the priest-astronaut's tenderness, the barking accountant's ferocity, the chemist-poet's hyena-like persistence.

10. The Neo-Decadent Man, not wanting his fashion to be thought of as inferior in audacity to that of his female counterpart, should be swift and bold in making sharp sartorial decisions, and at the same time not run the risk of presenting himself as a dandified clothes fetishist. He should strip himself of dirty denims and replace them with fabric that falls. Most importantly, he should be wary of stultifying trends and should not hesitate to clothe himself in heroic acts, even if in dull, domestic settings. A heavy regal crown-like turban bedecked with jewels, a large silver bracelet and a small dagger hidden beneath his shirt should be encouraged, even whilst taking a jaunt about town.

11. Historically, the military has driven much men's fashion. Intimately familiar with various campaigns of seduction, performance, and urban exploration—not to mention the creative ridicule and destruction of our enemies—we wish to transpose the elements of persuasion, infiltration and improvisation to our clothing, given that even our leisure has its strategic component. All preening, guilty and ruminative clothes must be cast off, so that our mere presence may pre-emptively decimate the dead edifices of academic guilds and fast fashion sweatshops.

12. As he navigates crowded urban centres, the Neo-Decadent Man should at all times be aware of his entire appearance—all constituent parts of his total ensemble—for at no point should he be compromised if a fellow passer-by makes reference to even a minor trinket he might have forgotten he had put on. His clothing should be light, in terms of both weight and colour. The traditional top-bottom two-piece ensemble should be replaced with a long flowing one-piece garment accentuated by accessories adorning the body's edges: hats and turbans, rings, bracelets and talismans on the edges of the hands. The feet may rest or slip into a slim, almost invisible pair of thin shoes to keep him perpetually alert.

13. Holy colours: gold, silver, pink, chrome yellow, forest green. Metallic harmonies, sharp contrasts, musical jewellery, gleaming devices.

14. The fashion cycle can be compared to ancient agricultural festivities that marked the change of seasons, festivities of death and renewal, so much so that every new garment, once worn, already begins to die. This explains why old fashions resurface. The Neo-Decadent Man may occasionally don a shirt reminiscent of a bygone trend, but not without the necessary ritual to bring the shirt back to life. It is forbidden to remove from your cupboard a shirt you wore in high school and put it on without this necessary ritual, without which the dead clothing must be discarded.

15. Walking through aisles of cheaply produced acrylic garments that lack all levity and bear no resonance with or relationship to the man wearing them, the Neo-Decadent Man will have to garner his own sense of style by conferring meaning to his collar, the fall of his pants or the motif on a cassock; his clothes will signify his psychic profile without conveying any arbitrary message. The working man will not dare arrive for a meeting in his white shirt and grey trousers coupled with a laptop bag. Men will have to appear striking, each in his own way, enhancing his physiognomy, but at no possible cost will two men appear remotely similar, in the manner of rancidly competent professionals arriving at a conference: all will appear distinct, as if comfortable in their own shells, their own cloth, and will conduct themselves accordingly.

16. The office will be altered not just by removing heavy oak furniture and oppressive carpeting, but by

a workers' movement—composed largely of working men—to break down all rules of vestimentary grammar. Women will not find it out of place to return to their luscious long hair of early youth; they will expose their midriffs in fractal pattern saris made of newly devised enduring fibre, whereas men will appear at the workplace in pale tunics, saffron kurtas, red kaftans and phirans. As a result, the office will no longer be defined by the garb of its own failure.

17. The notion of any age being beyond parody is itself ripe for parody. For fashion, parody functions as a disinfectant, and if employed properly, it produces novel beauty through defamiliarization. Neo-Decadence, when considered by passéists and the ill-informed, might sound like a contradiction: how can there be new decay, fresh declines? This becomes clearer when it is realized that our clothes embody the decadence not just of the storied past or insistent present, but of various parallel paths in time. At the crossroads, where the accelerated Empire meets the ruins of remote antiquity, we are setting up looms, studios, 3D printers, molecular assemblers; the peasant threading a bone needle works alongside the sartorial artist-scientist of the future who knits discardable masterpieces from the raw materials of space. As the future declines into the present, Neo-Decadence is born, and the Neo-Decadent Man stands askance, clad in thrift shop items from sideways in time: a wardrobe of resurrected trends and impossible hybrids; the clothes of cancelled histories.

18. A typical strategy: recuperation of speculative subcultures. The 1960s Tiki-Mod craze of Outer Mongolia, though unknown to our universe, provides us with the imaginative materials needed to extract garments from Ulaanbaatar death boys with rum mugs, volcano gloves and synthetic suede boots. Now rotate this trend through the Prussian military culture of the 1870s and a new crispness will emerge: the desperate revelry of imminent death, presided over by dapper, drunken tribal gods of the steppe. We can envision a Europe depopulated by the Black Death not in the Middle Ages, but in the 1970s; the tide of Islamic invaders would raid empty discotheques for sequined jumpsuits and flares. As the clothes produced become further estranged from their originating conceits, fashion will be cleansed, and real style will make itself known.

19. The Neo-Decadent Man will draw little inspiration from those ultimate passéists, plants and animals. How pitiful are the birds, who have never thought to invent plastic surgery. Parrots chatter like businessmen, secure in their naive vulgarity, while swans wander the grass like drunken louts, and egrets congregate colourlessly like Uniqlo customers. The same spirit that would rehabilitate the facial contours of a dove is the spirit we will prize in our Neo-Decadent aesthetic consultants.

20. Each man should dress like the unsuspected household god of an imaginary building.

COOKING

Brendan Connell
Justin Isis

The Decay of Dining

In past ages, the primary purpose of food was to fortify the body and to bring the spirit in closer contact with the gods. Today, however, through the decayed state of the social structure, its primary purpose, among all who are not starving, is to entertain and to declaim one's STATUS and to display a flaccid costume of COMMUNITY. The Neo-Decadents, instead of rejecting this sorry state, embrace it, shouting loudly from the cafés and rooftops to the crowded boulevards, summoning both the curious and the confounded.

Some exist on diets of cartilage, worms, or fried brains, while others sip dew from flowers and turn away from rancid flesh with disgust. All embracing, however, we are able to see the ULTIMATE in countless actions. We simply DEMAND WAKEFULNESS.

To eat is to kill. MURDERERS EVERYWHERE! We see them lunging at us, their lips wet with hunger, their eyes sharp with lust. Ever-abundant, we let them dine on us, on our sinews and ideas, on the music of our mouths and the smell of our loins.

Cooking must be taken outside the confines of the material world. The MIGHTY FRUIT is whipped up from ideas, from savage nightmares and whispering dreams. Recipes must be SHOCKING, and wine glasses full of the sweet blood of angels. Dining on over-exposed ragues and phosphorescent pies, in which rest unnamable meats and bizarre sinews, TRUE UNDERSTANDING AND SCIENCE EXPLODE!

Have you ever sautéed geometrical sex or eaten fate from the breasts of Minerva? AWAY WITH DISCRETION! The mirrors and crystals reflect tastes, the curtains are replete with rare pungencies. . . . MODERN COOKING MUST BE DESTROYED! WE WILL NEVER EAT FROM GIANT WHITE PLATES!

The enteric nervous system—the true seat of the soul—demands an appropriately slavering ministry. From the ENTERIC PULPIT we proclaim the need for recombinant recipes, aleatoric cooking. Rock salt rubbed on dripping flanks. Tapioca teas and spider cereal for newborn sorcerers.

NO MORE NUTRITIOUS SLIMES BLENDED AND CANNED! We dream of fruit-meats, candied vegetables, luminous vitamin-and-mineral ice. The utensil-claws of the future rending fleshy portals in the merely POSSIBLE.

RATS, CROWS AND COCKROACHES: true gourmands of the urban buffet. We leave the restaurants to them, taking our appetites elsewhere. The raw planes and angles of industrial coffins and financial towers will be converted into enormous picnic spreads, concrete tables laden with delicacies. When the electricity fails, it will be time for sentimental desserts: winter melons and youthful ambitions roasted in moonlight. We will PURGE OURSELVES OF MERE PHYSICAL HUNGER AND DINE IN THE LAPS OF IMPROVISED GODS.

The Vertical Table

We are used to encountering the table as a necrophile encounters a corpse: vulnerable in repose, courting decay. Everything is supine, limply accessible, liable to rot. This persistently two-dimensional arrangement has led us, like the sloppy enthusiast of the deceased, to embrace the most ghastly passivity. Dead matter arranges itself for our convenience in a horizontal tableau, without the bracing tonic of an active gravity. Resistance is necessary for tension and development, yet the modern table presents us with none: sluggish digestion results, and we leave as unsatisfied as we arrived.

Strictly considered, the horizontal table still indecently displayed in our homes is a relic of the 20th century, ill-suited to our current existence and spiritually reeking of a hospital ward in which any dribbling convalescent is welcome to bother us. Approaching the table, we start by lowering ourselves, submitting to chairs, which lock us in place (properly speaking, one defecates while seated or squatting, but one does not eat in this position, much less concern oneself with the psychic effluents of other consumers). Tedious mouths appear in space, and we pick and prod at bits of meat and pieces of plants— conveniently sectioned and segregated, drizzled with dressings—while fielding all manner of fatuous imposi- tions and maudlin reminiscences, the fortification of our flesh constantly interrupted by second-hand opinions, unsupportable politics and intolerable solicitations. Our spirits become flattened and distended as we chew, and our minds film over with a scum of sentiment. The whole thing usually ends with resigned indulgence in cheap wine, cocaine of dubious purity, desserts that are little more than defrosted clots of refined sugar, and whatever other palliatives are on hand. Televisions glower behind us, waiting like lampreys to attach their monitor-mouths to our postprandial weakness.

It is too much to hope for an expansive apartment or secluded estate. It is too much even to expect solitude. Most of us come to hunger surrounded by our lovers, our children, whatever conspirators and collaborators we deem necessary. But we must not let them interrupt our delectation, and we must not interrupt theirs. Rather, arrangements must be made to discourage talk and encourage focused consumption. The table must be reformulated: the supine corpse must spring to life and stand.

The vertical table need not be a luxury item. A simple sheet of metal will do: rectangular, firmly-supported, rising from floor to ceiling. The arrangement of dishes will resemble something an artful shrike might construct: delicacies fixed in place, impaled on spikes and pins. Various braziers may be inserted or suspended in place, heating the items directly above them, warming those around them with an ambient glow. More elaborate tables with sliding sections will become glorious culinary cabinets resembling a lady's bureau, packed with compartments full of exotic condiments and unexpected side dishes. Circumambulation of the table will reveal new angles from which to consider the relationships between items, new perspectives on their improvised yet integrated system.

The vertical table: the meal as Ascension, as focused conquest. Each item, pinned in place, will draw attention to those above it, encouraging a simple, timely progression and eliminating the need for multiple courses with oppressive cutlery and superfluous dishes. One might start with earthy staples—potatoes, perhaps—easily accessible at waist level, before moving on to the animal flesh and vegetables situated above them, at last arriving at airier, sweeter delights in the higher regions. The abolition of plates will allow for immediate correspondences between items, sudden and shifting constellations of flavour. The juice from a ripe mandarin may drip onto a bit of lightly-seared steak, while chillies, artfully sliced, scatter seeds of fire on the sliced apples below, and cubes of skewered pork slide into votive bowls of raw yolk: vitalizing emanations; novel configurations of sour and savoury, hot and cold. The system of the meal will stand revealed with all its subtle interconnections.

It is best to dine on utterly fresh meats and vegetables and to serve them mostly raw. We suggest:

> A bull's heart on a spike, drizzled with lemon juice.
> Oysters, gently agitated so that they threaten to slip from their shells.
> Thinly-sliced salmon and tuna, acquainted with white pepper.
> A ball of mozzarella, pinioned, obese.
> Figs and dates, dusted with cocoa.
> A fan of livers.
> Candied pineapple.
> Rose petals.
> Fried information.
> Curtains of tripe.
> Roasted crickets.
> Diverse fermented notions.
> Salted lobster tails.
> Wasp honey.
> Wine-soaked watermelon.

Vintage prayers.

A cleansing sorrow, the consistency of shaved ice.

Desserts should be placed in the uppermost reaches of the table, barely within reach: cinnamon sticks; small speared tarts; saucers of cream with floating raspberries, liable to spill on the heads of the unwary and unfocused who lack the dexterity to reach them. Mashed pears. Pomegranate ice cream.

The attitude of approach is essential; one should be hungry enough to pluck the eyes from a deer in mid-leap. It should be necessary not only to stand, but to strain one's arms upward, seizing delicacies as if from the branches of a steel tree, forcing the aspirational posture of a mendicant reaching for sustenance: eating while standing, while moving, while dancing. Conversation should mostly be discouraged, or limited to discussion of which items to taste next. Screens of all kinds should be banished: there is nothing more revolting than a roomful of stuffed spectators gnawing on bland nonsense while numbed by the latest serial drama or streaming inanity.

The horizontal table: lethargy; the Fall; assumption of the Death Posture while feeding. The vertical table: lightness, liberation and athleticism: a return to active physical engagement.

The vertical table: prime rampart of the Neo-Decadent fortress of consumption: also improvised gallery wall, anatomical exhibition of vitalizing forces.

We will resurrect the corpse of the table as a shining monument to our own appetites. Passéists still dining horizontally will be mocked and shunned as ghoulish throwbacks.

Standing erect, we will embrace the luxurious rapacity of our existence, so that we may grow strong and breed as all ravenous things must: locusts; missionaries; dissenting opinions; sunflowers with bright brown faces and crowns of insolent gold, their spirits those of drunken jesters mocking the ugly solemn sky.

Household Hints

Meals can be colour-coded.

Keep company with those who are cheerful, those who suck on pears as if they were wounds, and who pronounce their sexual urges as if they were laws.

Supply guests with a single huge spoon each, regardless of what is being served. This is the best way to stop them from talking about their struggles during meal time.

Avoid things that are overly relaxing, such as warm rooms and soft mattresses.

One should cut bread with a knife that has been used for suicide.

Dining in a solitary hut is the summit of extravagance.

Appropriate incense should be lit to regulate the mood. The air can be cleansed by burning buttons of peyote.

For dinner parties, at least two or three madmen should be included amongst the company, those who will mutilate their food as they eat it, and spit on the table as their eyes roll around in their heads as others nibble on their thumbs with uncertain anxiety.

There is nothing more revolting than to see wine drunk out of goblets or glasses.

Brisk wines should be served in *tazzini*, and drunk with a counter-point of gravity, in the manner of Abyssinian priests.

Honey can ritualistically be rubbed over the cup before drinking.

To demonstrate vocation, white wine can be flavoured with cowslips.

When offering someone a dish, pronounce its name with a lisp.

If one cannot garnish a dish with pearls or emeralds, one should not garnish it at all.

One should always keep a remedy for excitement near the dinner table.

Never whisper.

Never wash dishes with soap, as then everything will taste like soap.

Place a container of rhubarb powder on the table in the place of pepper. Black pepper is revolting and should never be eaten, even by the most transgressive.

Rise up early every morning and wash the eyes in rose water.

The only thing black pepper is good for is killing flies.

Many people like vomit, so never expect to be appreciated.

The German method for preventing excitement is the most efficacious.

MUSIC

Ramón Alanís

1. Synaesthesia.

2. The ardour of our Song shall not be quenched by profit, awards, media exposure, or any romantic notions of posterity. It shall burn until our very body is down to embers.

3. If a chord progression and a melody are a naked body, pleasing as some human forms can be, it is the arrangements that constitute its garments. Our music will not wear the same uniform every time, but require brand new attires with different colours, textures, shapes and ornaments fitting to each occasion or appearance.

4. Technical perfection is not desirable. After Heraclitus: *no man ever performs the same piece twice.*

5. The concept of "genre" is a convenient label for stocking products at stores and for casual description, but serves no practical purpose for creative and artistic

endeavours. We will combine styles and forms to suit our fancy, break things apart to salvage and repurpose the useful pieces.

6. Perverse individuals believe music theory to be a shackle to their creativity, limiting them to established forms and formulas, discouraging experimentation or the pushing of any boundaries. Throw their words into a bottomless pit, for it is musicians that do not study music who keep repeating and imitating the only formulas they know. Music theory is at once a dissection toolset and a sledgehammer.

7. The old adage says "great artists steal," but just stealing will not make you an artist, let alone a great one. Reinvention, reinterpretation, recontextualization are key. Instead of copying or sampling, rewrite the music in reverse, or apply negative harmony to its melody. Decompose and recompose it with modal jazz reharmonization. Use it as a counterpoint to your own music. There are as many ways to steal as there are things to steal.

8. The Neo-Passéist tends to "reinvigorate" styles of yore by imbuing them with modernity (electro swing, punk cabaret, synthwave, psychobilly, Postmodern Jukebox and their many imitators, etc.) If one must look into the past for ideas or influences, it shall be done not out of nostalgia but with the contemptible sordidness of a graverobber or the investigative rigeur of a pathologist.

9. There was a man in Africa whose leg was amputated; he had his tibia fashioned into a flute by a skilled luthier and made it his instrument. Music is, in one way or another, sacrificial.

10. The verse-chorus form: an archaic relic as despicable as the three-arc story structure. Existing between the simplicity of minimalism and the complex intricacies of a modernist concert work, our music structures will be culled from the inscrutable logic of dreams, weather patterns in foreign regions, a series of scents we pass on the street, the architecture of foreign temples, the folds in the clothes of our beloved . . . Repetition legitimises, but discontinuance can reinforce too.

11. There should not be much emphasis on lyrics. A song should be worth listening to even if the audience does not understand the words, or if there aren't any. As practice, become accustomed to music from languages you can not understand, and do not try to understand it by the context of its music video or by translating the lyrics. When you write lyrics, strive for poetry and transcend the anecdotal or autobiographical. Write different sets of lyrics for the same song and alternate them each performance, or attempt glossolalia at your leisure.

12. Our music will not be created with an intimate gathering, street-busking, a club, a theatre or music hall, let alone stadiums or sports arenas in mind. If we intend to reach new heights, we must compose as if our music is going to be performed in the most bizarre and exquisite contexts: at brothels in ruins, over forest fires, at execu-

tions, on forlorn roads, at sky burials, at a congress of demiurges, at an agalmatophilic orgy...

13. Discern which ideas should be expressed in a grandiose manner, and which would be spoiled by fleshing them out too much. Without striving towards minimalism, sometimes simplicity is key.

14. We will embrace the dissonant, the offbeat, the microtonal, the angular. When it comes to music production, we reject digital quantization and will fight against the Loudness War from our trenches.

15. Finally, Neo-Decadent musicians will compose their own requiems. For we ignore where life will lead us, but do know how it ends.

ARCHITECTURE

Damian Murphy
Gaurav Monga
LC von Hessen

1. Architecture is a necessary lie, an essential perversion of the prodigality of nature, a crucial mistake, an imperative ruse, and the most fortuitous of scandals. Every one of our predecessors has laboured under a single, unfortunate error—they failed to develop the hidden iniquities of an art that defies utility.

2. Although the Neo-Decadents can appreciate old, and even ancient architecture—they adore the temple walls of Hampi and Khajuraho, for example—they view with suspicion the constant desire to recast the new to appear as if it were old. In fact, nothing stops them from admiring falling-apart façades and parapets. Wooden, intricately ornate doors of old havelis sold in the marketplace for cheap offer us a sense of violent joy and even relief, for we embrace decay, demolition, and even disaster in order to pave way for the new.

3. The aesthetic of shiny, loud banality that characterizes

the 21st century must be cast off like dead skin, twisted into arcane knots, and publicly set alight. In particular, the ultracapitalist sense of interior design that gears itself towards hypothetical future real estate sales potentially decades down the line, towards generic figures parasitically projecting their own banal ideals into one's own living space, has reached its nadir in the vogue for hyperminimalism: the padded cell of upwardly-mobile wealth in shades of taupe and beige dictated by one's local Homeowners' Association.

4. We will dispense with the Modernists once and for all with their featureless boxes of concrete and glass. It's best to pretend that they never existed and begin again from first principles. We must restore the importance of aesthetics, yet this is merely a portion of the architect's art. As for function, our principal aim is to subvert the poetics of space.

5. The Neo-Decadent Architect understands that interior decor must be pleasing to the eye, and all other senses, in disparate combinations of the beautiful and grotesque. One's living space should resemble one's psyche splayed out on the walls, just as the heavily-tattooed body serves as a living house of flesh and bone.

6. Far-left starkly-utilitarian "anti-elitist" architecture has much more in common with far-right nostalgic propaganda kitsch architecture than it would like to believe—and vice versa. We must advance an architec-

ture of catastrophe, because Brutalism is not enough. If architecture is frozen music, we must push it one step further into frozen noise. Our floor plans will prove to be mathematically impossible; our facades an affront to common sense. No single room will be accessible from any other and our corridors will be bent into spirals.

7. We'll build a house of lies the likes of which has never been uttered before. Our carpets will confound, our lamps conceal, our passages obstruct, and our locks will be unfaithful. We'll let the night creep in through a crack in the foundation and impersonate the night watch. Even the shadows will revolt against the light—they'll cluster around it like a company of thieves.

8. The Neo-Decadents are wary of being encased in old tired walls for long winter months, which is why we prefer warmer climates where the architecture of living rooms spills out onto the streets, into bazaars and open courtyards, places to celebrate. We like to take strolls on the footpaths of wide bridges carrying people and goods from the new city to the old; there we devour kebabs, large breads and black tea out of samovars served to us on the street on plastic stools. The buildings around us are either old and failing with multiple entrances, old roofs—too old to be restored—or one can already see the construction site of a shopping mall. On the streets we have men dressed in shirt and tie, Salwar-Kameez and an occasional fakir or baba emerging entirely naked.

9. Buildings will no longer be dwelling places, homes, but sites of trespass and unending futile mystery featuring secret vaults, rooms opening into each other without purpose or plan, or staircases leading into ceilings. In our new homes, we will rarely see familiar faces, unless by sheer accident. As a result, family structures will be, by the sheer weight of their dismantled architecture, torn apart and reduced to debris. Here, everyone will squat in anonymous rooms of fully developed apartment complexes or even construction sites, rooms that can be at any moment ransacked and evacuated even while you are sleeping in them at night. You may fall asleep in one room and find yourself in a room of some other building when you awake.

10. Neo-Decadent architecture will not be built. There will be no effort, no plans, no laborers, no brick or mortar. These buildings will come into being on their own, effortlessly, like a magic trick, a theatre of surprise.

11. Our architecture will be based largely on the prospect of play. Stairs spiralling endlessly towards an empty attic, the fun of which being the resultant vertigo. The kitchen will be full of gargantuan pots and pans, large spoons the size of a fully grown man hanging on a small wooden door.

12. The most important features of any house or structure are precisely those that can not be detected without either taking the structure apart or subjecting it to a thorough investigation. These features must be hidden

with exceeding care, with the intent of exerting an effect on the occupants in a far more profound way than mere ornamentation or convenience. Blueprints and floor plans can be subtly falsified in order to conceal all evidence of these elements. Their chief quality, and most essential virtue, lies precisely in their invisibility.

13. Any house of reasonable size should be equipped with a hidden central chamber whose location and dimensions can only be deduced by a close examination of the surrounding areas. So long as the room isn't overly large, very few will come to suspect its existence, yet it will be sensed beneath the surface of the conscious mind and will come to attain an almost religious significance. Likewise, more modest spaces can be concealed in the interstices between rooms and corridors. These should be embellished with incongruous décor, which, were they ever discovered, would dazzle the senses. The effect will be all the more poignant for the fact that few, if any, will ever lay eyes on them.

14. Likewise, spaces that don't exist can be referred to in official specifications. This must always be done with the utmost casualness and never with consistency. Reference might be made to a 'relay room' in a veterinary hospital or a 'memetic chamber' in a school for the blind. Care must be taken to ensure that this is never done directly, but rather mentioned in passing while documenting another part of the building. A network of dumbwaiters, secret doors, one-way mirrors, and crawl spaces might be included in a blueprint but never actually built. If carried

out properly, these will be purely symbolic and will reveal something of the soul of the structure.

15. This brings us to the next point—the subtle architecture of the inner planes. Every house or building has an etheric double that comprises its true foundation. This is a natural condition of conventional architecture and arises on its own without the builder's knowledge. The Neo-Decadent Architect, on the other hand, will work this into their design. By rites and protocols known only to them, or handed down through a succession of anonymous hands, they'll fashion a framework on the visionary planes before work on the floor plan has begun. Subtle anomalies can be introduced in defiance of known geometrical laws. This will give rise to any number of features, the least of which will reveal themselves in the dreams of the inhabitants.

16. For most, these new buildings will represent their last hope. The Neo-Decadents, however, scoff at this perverse fetish of building new designs as a symbol of a surviving civilization. Instead, we endorse ruin, and feel sick in overly sanitized, clinical architecture. Even today's restaurants are beginning to look like modern hospitals. Our notion of architecture has less to do with building than with destroying, until there are very few buildings left. Throughout the construction of the building the workers must at all times feel that they are taking something apart. Either we destroy or silently watch buildings fall to ruin of their own accord.

17. The effort spent in constructing as opposed to destroying may already at the very outset appear futile, for even when detailed blueprints are made, these buildings somehow never come to fruition, no matter how hard the architects and workers labour. Once erected, these buildings always look the same, a mere facade of the blueprint; the workers always find that the fallen bricks they collect from the rubble are never the same ones they used in construction.

18. The Neo-Decadent must exploit the psychology that underlies the division of space, tilting the odds toward the irrational act that redeems the sin of limitation. Through the careful management of the ratios found in every aspect of a building, certain vital essences can be concentrated at key points in the interior. If handled correctly, this can lead to a series of cathartic psychic eruptions. This has long been taken advantage of in the theatre and the opera house—why not an embassy, a hotel, or a notary's office as well? To foment this type of catastrophic ecstasy in the institutions of the bourgeoisie would at once revitalize society and exalt the architect's art.

19. Opportunities to place a weapon in the hand of fate are manifold. Spyholes can be strategically installed to encourage the proliferation of dangerous knowledge, floors tilted to an imperceptible degree to cause an ambience of vertigo, the occasional door should lock from the outside just as a single window on an upper story

should be impossible to close. All of these techniques are secondary to the subtler aspects of the craft—perplexing inconsistencies of light and shadow, a deliberate confusion of boundaries, the persistent feeling that a space is larger on the inside than its exterior would suggest, and the displacement of physicality such that the inhabitants feel out of sync with their environment. Luxuriant comfort should be intermingled with an unshakable sense of unease to give rise to an incredible range of sensations that make our current interiors seem bland. Crime, being central to the human experience, must not be neglected in the structures we inhabit. If the modern home has robbed us of a portion of our humanity, we must take it back by force.

20. The plans of a building will from the outset allow for an element of danger, even the possibility of getting severely injured. Schools will be constructed with playgrounds where children may accidentally assault one another without meaning to and in which sometimes, as a result of some unintended slight, physical fights will ensue. Neo-Decadence cannot avoid the prospect of actively seeking an architecture of danger as a sort of balm. To know that at any moment you may disappear into the debris as a result of an intentional flaw in the building's essential blueprint is indispensable.

21. Our tenement buildings, also, will be replete with the most fabulous of perils—wolves will rush up and down the stairwells, rapacious birds will swarm through

the elevator shafts, secret springs of wine and molasses will bubble up through fissures in the basement floor. A haunting chorus of idiot savants will be heard at certain hours of the night, their imbecilic songs reverberating through the heating vents while their precise location can never be determined. The entire structure will be built to rotate on several different axes, causing irreparable damage to the furnishings and posing a constant threat to the tenants. Those that survive the fruits of our whimsy will emerge with hidden knowledge of the House of Fate, that masterpiece of architecture to which even the most seasoned builder can only aspire.

22. Neo-Decadence scoffs at the architecture of utility and the resultant modern nuclear family. Notions of privacy, simplicity, sobriety must be immediately discarded—so much so that you can expect to walk into someone's bedroom as an entry point to a new apartment and, after having crossed many layers of architectural fold, find that the living room is hidden in a corner. Neo-Decadent architecture references the labyrinths of ancient Greece even before they assumed structural forms, existing as a dancing ritual of teenage boys and girls and later as the Roman rites performed for the purpose of founding a new city. There is no single method to enter or exit our buildings, for these are labyrinths whose architecture rests not only on many folds but can also be folded in many ways.

23. The city functions as haunted house writ large. Echoes of years, decades, centuries of past turmoil and jubilance

etch themselves into façades and sidewalks, fencing and statuary. The enterprising Neo-Decadent becomes a midnight flâneur, a wandering observer of the secrets of the City, folding oneself into a silent set of senses drifting alone down side streets and crossroads and public transit hubs to mentally catalogue the detritus of our times, the clues left unwittingly by unknown lives.

24. One must become cognizant of the Spectral Mirror of the City, the mind-palace of the collective unconscious, revealing in dream alone the great promise of what the urban landscape might have become. E.g. Manhattan rendered as a tight-yet-sprawling mass of Boschian spires in the iridescent texture of abalone shells and enormous silver statues half-sunken into the sea, transversed by a looping roller coaster of a monorail. Massive windows reveal equally-massive brass gears rotating human-sized clockwork devils and mannequins for the wonder of passers-by.

25. The modern cityscape has fitfully smashed its ca-thedrals into a cluster of soulless stripped bone shards jutting from the barren earth, all embellishment shorn off and swept away like butchers' and barbers' leavings. Entire walls made of windows remain coldly uncovered, that anyone might stare from below or across into one's doings: an aesthetic of passive surveillance. The Neo-Decadent Architect must resurrect the damask and velvet curtain, the glimmer of lamplight through a dis-creetly-glimpsed keyhole, the lush occult maximalism of the cloak-and-dagger.

26. Most of us will prefer to sleep outside, for buildings—most buildings, spaces of domestic care and strife—will be viewed with disdain and apprehension; homes, the stuff families are made of will soon begin to reek with a stench of domestic quarrel and will emerge ubiquitously in the future as large traps. We will soon begin to look at all architecture with suspicion and will avoid entering buildings, avoid prospects of setting up family units and fathering/mothering children who will look like us, who will grow up in rooms not so dissimilar from the ones we grew up in. Instead, we will pitch tents and have intercourse with whomever we find, our moment's love. In case of an earthquake, we will disappear with our belongings before the buildings crash to the ground.

27. Our buildings will be holey spaces, fragments not part of larger constellations or building complexes, but stand-alone structures that resemble ruins, the only difference being that these buildings will not slowly decline into ruin with the passage of time but will rise into ruins even before they are constructed. We often arrive in buildings, just as we arrive in cities, accidentally, and sometimes cannot leave.

28. The pure, unmarked blueprint is in every way perfect. Every design is a blemish, every line a fatal flaw. To build is to destroy the mathematical perfection of the one-dimensional point. Every house is a sin in three dimensions, every building is a misdeed. The Neo-Decadent architect not only embraces this truth but pushes it to its limit.

29. Our once-noble art lies abandoned and depraved in the wilderness of academia. The Seven Lamps of Architecture left us by John Ruskin have long since gone out in the desolate night. Blind, intoxicated, naked, and deranged, we must erect a new scaffolding in the dark. We'll proceed entirely by accident and necromancy, kindling the flames of seven infernos: Bombast, Duplicity, Mimicry, Seduction, Prophecy, Subtext, and Oblivion. These will be our principles, seven in number, of which the eighth cannot be named.

30. Our predecessors number in the very few: Piranesi, M. C. Escher, Paul Laffoley, Sarah Winchester, Raymond Roussel, Brodsky & Utkin, and Maurice Blanchot. There are others, though we dare not name them, while still others are anonymous or entirely unheard of. The most scandalous of architects will never be known, their influence as invisible as it is ubiquitous.

IMMATERIALISM

Quentin S. Crisp

1. Materialism is the poisonous sump from which all evil spreads. It is the ultimate chauvinism of the soulless.

2. The materialist insists on judging all others by his own deficiency. He calls his littleness common sense and his resentment rationality.

3. And what is matter? The ultimate Rorschach test. The materialist is truly only someone who insists on a particular interpretation or nuance of matter. Let us psychoanalyse that interpretation, that nuance. Matter represents the termination of thought. It 'just is'. One way of saying 'just is' is 'brute fact'; another is 'magic'. All of these can stand in place of the x that matter is. x = just is; x = brute fact; x = magic. We show the materialist the Rorschach x and for intriguing, hidden reasons he avoids the last of these responses. Let us winkle out the reasons. Let us use 'magic' interchangeably with 'brute fact' like beaters intent on scaring game into the open.

4. The general idea of materialism that the materialist wishes to affirm is a myth abstracted from the limited data of a former age. It is a ghost that haunts science—a ghost of circular logic. Is materialism simply the final description of our actual universe? But we don't have the final description. Even supposing we had it, would any universe diverging from that description in any way therefore be supernatural? If so, almost all universes that are logically possible defy materialism, and we just happen to live in a materialist universe—you might say by definition, since materialism is supposedly defined by the conjectured 'right' description of the universe we happen to live in. In other words, in such a case, there is nothing at all to preclude the non-materialist possibilities that simply did not happen to form in this universe. Materialists, of course, dislike the idea that there could have been any universe but this. One might begin to wonder what it is about this indefinable materialism that makes them wish to insist on it. Meanwhile the artist wanders in all that is conceivable.

5. Matter can only ever be a springboard—a jumping off point for what is important. It is the MacGuffin of the universe. At least, as long as it is defined as whatever is not mental, this is so, and the only alternative is the dead end of saying that there is nothing mental. In which case there is only x, after all. And we are back to the question, what is x? (Magic, remember!) But returning to the inscrutable conventions of traditional 'matter'—matter is never important in itself for the very simple reason that importance is not material.

6. If you come to the dead end that is matter, what then? You are positively compelled to go beyond it.

7. Some people claim to know what matter forbids, in the same way that others claim to speak for God. There is at least one difference: matter cannot make any moral claims. If matter cannot force me to restrain my imagination from this or that direction, it cannot command me to, either. Therefore, the prophets of matter must either abandon reason or remain silent.

8. Meanwhile, the artist is a conjuror, producing from his sleeve the most fantastical things possible. "See. Whatever matter is, it allows me to do this. And this. And this."

9. What we call 'fantasy' is not the only artistic tool against materialism. The opposite tool, too, can be used—what has been called 'naturalism'. Karl Jaspers writes: "anyone who philosophizes strives for scientific knowledge, for it is the only way to achieve genuine non-knowledge, it is as though the most magnificent insights could be achieved only through man's quest for the limit at which cognition runs aground." In other words, exhaust the phenomena and you will be presented with the remainder—the beyond, freedom, the spirit. So in art, chip away everything but the phenomena and by contrast that within which the phenomena are suspended will become clearer and clearer.

10. The atheist stands before the vast door beyond which lies eternity. It is open a crack, but he refuses to push at it. The materialist stands before the opalescent door behind which the spirit moves. It is open a crack, but he shrugs and declines to look inside. "It's probably nothing."

11. This supposed indifference is a ruse. "Who cares about eternity? That slut?! Just look at all the priests and mystics and other parasites she's had before we could get anywhere near her!"

12. The concept is a strange interface between entity and cipher. The materialist strives always to reduce entity to cipher via concept. We must never forget the proper direction of flow is the reverse of this. We learn the ciphers so that we might pin down concepts and make them portable, and the concepts, correctly studied, are prisms which, when they receive the light of our consciousness, ray it out into colourful entity.

13. Is it, in fact, strangeness that the materialist fears? Contemporary philosophical discourse, which strives towards an elusive materialism as towards a rainbow's end, is replete with references to the 'spooky', meaning anything that cannot easily be explained within the materialist rubric. Do they want a universe entirely devoid of spookiness? What could this mean? As Lafcadio Hearn observes, even science turns us into "ghosts of ourselves". Do they wish to sit in the drabbest of roadside cafes eating the drabbest of sandwiches? Would that reassure them? But even a sandwich can be spooky. Jack

Kerouac hints at this with his concept of the naked lunch moment: "a frozen moment when everyone sees what is on the end of every fork." Or, in this case, the moment you really taste the entity that fills your sandwich.

14. The materialist, in other words, wants his sandwich fully dressed, in the conceptual equivalent of the suit and tie. He wants a world in which lunch never disrobes. One can almost begin to sympathise with this metaphysical prudery, since it makes the Dance of the Seven Veils by which Being gradually reveals itself that much more enticing.

15. The spooky is the gateway to the numinous. There is a borderland of the spooky where clocks and watches go haywire. There are other manifestations, but these are too numerous to list. At some point, the passage into the Underworld is always necessary. You sign a waiver at the entrance. You fall. You buy a one-way ticket on the ghost train, unsure of your return. "Abandon control, all ye who enter here."

16. You fall into the nightmare, as in a dream of falling from a cliff—into it, and through it. You are falling down, but at some point you fall to the very core of spookiness, and then you begin to fall up.

17. Ultimately, whether he says so or not, whether he knows it or not, the materialist is for control and against freedom.

18. Even his desire for control is self-contradictory and self-undermining. Materialism, giving supremacy to physical cause and effect, results in determinism. The materialist, seeking to control through physical cause and effect—ultimately to control all things—is, if his philosophy be true, in fact only controlled.

19. The idea has been put forward that the human brain can be engineered—genetically or otherwise—in such a way that the subject will always act morally. This is argued with a materialist presumption of determinism, but the idea contains a glaring fallacy that illustrates well the materialist's perpetual self-blindness.

20. Let us imagine a chain of arrows that is physical cause and effect, with environment part of this chain, affecting the brain and causing further effects of behaviour which in turn affect the environment. The idea is that interfering with the brain segment of the chain will bring about overall improvements. But from where do these presumed improvements come? The scientist who tampers with the brain for the sake of making moral improvements is himself, by his own account, only a part of another such unending chain. From inside the chain of cause and effect how can we be interfering agents of improvement to cause and effect? The scientist's actions in this scenario are at odds with his stated or implicit philosophy. Either he unconsciously considers himself beyond his own philosophy—an exception—or he is a conscious hypocrite and manipulator.

21. Whichever it is, unconscious superiority in the desire to control others, or conscious hypocrisy and manipulation, it is the task of the artist to take the antimaterialist position and shatter the psychological traps of the materialist.

22. Morality is linked to free will. There can be no morality without the presupposition of free will. Morality is also both what challenges free will and what gives it the weight of significance. An individual artist might focus, through art, especially on freedom or especially on morality, but each implies the other, and so the archetypal artist is engaged in dramatizing a Socratic dialogue between freedom and morality. None of this is possible for the materialist without disqualifying him as such.

23. By the principles of materialism, the mind should be something that can be materially constructed. To build a mechanical mind is, by the lights of the materialist, to prove materialism. The strategic importance to the materialist is clear; he thinks that mind is the very gap where the God of the Gaps takes refuge, like a hunted spiritual terrorist. But the human mind can grasp things that cannot be encoded. Humans can think beyond—or before—first principles, as mystics throughout history have attested in detail and as ordinary people demonstrate each day. In contrast, any programmed intelligence is entirely bound by the principles of its programming. Even if we read the same page, the computer and we, the computer is trapped on the page; we understand it by what is off the page. However much we 'show our work-

ings', our true workings cannot be shown. No consistent system can demonstrate its own consistency, says one of Gödel's incompleteness theorems. The system is the page. We, who are outside the page, reading it, live in that greater incompleteness.

24. The artist, then, must specialise in what comes before first principles—the entity before the concept—thus keeping ahead of the curse laid upon culture by Turing and his fallacious 'test'.

25. Alan Turing, with his Turing Machine, which stops dead when it comes to the answer to a question, created the template for our age; Alan Turing, the poster boy of superficiality.

26. The whole Turing paradigm is based on the fallacy that seems = is. But seems ≠ is. Under Turing's influence, the world prefers concept to entity and cipher to concept. Let us return to the living entity before life reaches the irreversible, meaningless answer given by the machine, and halts.

27. For those of us inclined to philosophy, the problem we must now turn to is that intractable and neglected problem of other minds. Turing assumed that we cannot confirm the existence of other minds. His test begins with resignation on the question of other minds. When we know for sure that there are other minds than our own, the Turing Test, which makes fakes of us all, will finally become obsolete.

28. The great gamble of art is that there are other minds, that solipsism is false. Turing does not take this gamble. He only says that there seem to be other minds and his goal is that a computer will seem as well as a human seems. Art presupposes something beyond the seeming. One way of expressing the matter is this: an artist must operate on the principle that a purely mental event, leaving no physical trace, is indeed an event.

29. The reader's interpretation is free, but only as free as any person's interpretation is of any other's speech. In other words, the author is not dead. The cut-up experiment might have had some interesting results, but it was solipsistic. We derive meaning from art because we assume it to be a communication of some kind. This is precisely the problem of other minds. This is why those who care about art and about the spirit must now be cognisant of this problem.

30. We have become used to the convergence of the human and the automaton. Many Internet bots are more articulate than many humans simply because of the decay of thought and expression in the latter. Therefore, there now exist many humans who would not pass the Turing Test. This is ironic in itself, but there is a further irony. As the numbers of such people increase they must surely approach a tipping point after which their increase becomes their decrease. That is, they will increase and decrease at one and the same time. This paradox is

possible because, since the judgement as to who passes the Turing Test will rely more and more on others like themselves, they will begin to pass the test again in greater numbers.

31. In this way we can see that many things are lost and excluded simply because the mind has lost the ability to accommodate them. This is the materialist project—to shrink the imaginative capacity of the mind until we are lost in a state of being unable to remember or imagine what we have lost. The artist, then, in exercising the imagination and expanding the mind's capacity, works to reverse this process and combat the materialist project, to switch our direction from a downward to an upward spiral.

32. Why is reductionism considered a virtue? To eliminate the senses would also be a form of reductionism. Someone blind from birth could exist very well without believing there is a possible sense he does not possess. If a sighted person tried to describe vision to him, on reductionist principles he should reject this information. The world is coherent without it. We could say, "The world is not so complicated that we need the sense of sight in order to explain it." The artist, on the other hand, is open to all data, including those of the spirit and of the imagination. This latter kind might even be thought of as created data—whatever the universe allows the artist to create.

33. How do we know there is free will? By using it.

34. Buridan's ass stands between two identical piles of hay equidistant from him. It is asked how, without free will, he might choose between these piles of hay and escape starvation. What if these two piles of hay were, on the one hand, 'free will exists' and on the other 'free will does not exist'? And suppose that they are identical and equidistant from the ass in this sense: the evidence for and against each is equally compelling. Then the ass must choose the pile 'free will exists' and break the stalemate. In choosing it he demonstrates it. This is art.

35. Let us end by saying that materialism does not allow us to appreciate even matter—whatever that weird cipher might be. We repeat, materialism is only really a restricted view of what matter is, designed to ward off the amorphous 'spookiness' which is, in itself, as indefinable as matter. We might do well to call in the psychologists to puzzle out the psychological meaning of 'matter' and 'spookiness' (each apparently only defined in opposition to the other) in order to find the real solution to this conundrum.

Materialism, anyway, seems, in practice, bound up with power—epistemic and technological. It values power rather than matter, and matter, being manipulable, is merely the means to power. The devastation caused to the material world—that is, the environment, for instance—in the pursuit of immaterial power—that is, money, whose physical existence is only the symbol for an immaterial, conceptual power—is an apt illustration of this.

Really to value the material world, we must abandon the materialism that fetishizes measurement, which is a philia for the domination and the degradation that the bondage of mere measurement brings to matter.

OCCULTISM

Damian Murphy

0. Our true manifesto has been thrice forgotten, inscribed anew in invisible ink, converted, with errors, into 6-bit ASCII, and archived via teletype onto candy-coloured punch tape. Fragments have surfaced in the bowels of Usenet, though key phrases have been altered and the names of God transposed. What follows is an attempt at reconstruction—*caveat emptor.*

1. The Invisible Kingdom stands naked before us beneath a harsh and unflattering light. What was once held sacred has been systematically defiled by the glare of ten thousand fluorescent bulbs. In our thirst for comprehension, we've disgraced the inmost Mystery. The consummation of the sacred marriage between the aspirant and the Holy One has been reduced to little more than an interrogation. Hope is not entirely lost, however. Despite the ubiquity of our surveillance, much yet remains concealed from us. When our most cherished institutions have exfoliated in the light, the only course of action left is to creep back into the shadows.

2. With some notable exceptions, the past several decades of occult advancement have yielded little more than disappointment. Nothing is more tedious than the solipsism of the left-hand path or the popular resurgence of "tradition". The Nietzsche-ization of Victorian Masonry has settled into a holding pattern of quiet desperation. Chaos magick was a spectacular flop, worth little more than a footnote. Occulture is the opium of the masses—the less ink spilled on its behalf, the better. In order to return to a more reasonable arcanum, we must proceed to the truly obscure.

3. Our holy books will be legion and of staggering variety: instruction booklets for console games that never reached the market, infomercials for sketchy investments recorded onto Betamax cassettes, wallpaper motifs culled from 1960s Belgian catalogues, and blueprints drafted by architects whose ambitions eclipsed their means. In these ephemeral relics can be found the gates to hidden palaces of initiatory splendour. One needs only be so clever as to find the means of ingress.

4. The detritus of a culture fallen into regression is the ideal mirror for the face of God. What better stone for the builders to reject than something so obsolete as to escape official notice? The wasteland of the 20th century is nothing less than a reliquary. Those that came before us have left in their wake an empire of exquisite jewels.

5. The likes of broken down amusement parks and Soviet-era video arcades are especially pliable to Neo-Decadent ends. The skeletal remains of a mould-consumed roller coaster are a veritable chapel of the Mysteries. The enterprising necromancer might ply their trade in the evacuated playgrounds of Pripyat, while the theurgically-inclined can pursue apotheosis in the ruined bordellos of the Golden Triangle.

6. There's little to be gained from profaning our temples with icons at the margins of popular culture. Only the thoroughly cast out, deleted, or forgotten can attain to the status of the sacred. To seek after the Divine is like hunting rare vinyl in the Ministry of State Security in Pyongyang. The more impossible the task, the more desirable the result. We're far more likely to invoke an anonymous civil servant from a forgotten principality under the House of Hohenzollern than the elder gods of Lovecraft. We must turn our backs on consumerist kitsch and learn to re-embrace the arcane.

7. The Neo-Decadent Occultist eschews practical magic in favour of heedless mysticism. We're prone to tying ourselves to the masts of our ships, setting the sails majestically aflame, invoking the sirens by their secrets names and epithets, and letting their abysmal wails usher us straight into the arms of God. Absolution must be sought in the most fabulous exceptions, just as Christ finds a home in the heretic's heart. The Catholic Church has always maintained that redemption lies in sin. We

should push this principle to its absolute limits and daz-zle the eyes of the Creator.

8. Renouncing the feasibility of our deepest aspirations is not enough—we must wield our flaming torches against the darkness of utility. We'll court extravagance to ensure that we remain forever in the red, for only in insolvency might we appeal to an Absolute that negates its emana-tions. If the saint spends every waking hour in the flame of their devotion, the Neo-Decadent sleeps in the eye of an inferno. We'll renounce our oblivion only when the night has been consumed.

9. Above all else, we must fiercely resist the temptation to simplify our work. The Neo-Decadent Occultist is far more akin to a bureaucratic expert than to a DIY ma-gician. The proclamations of our oracles must rival the complexity of international law. The work of John Dee and Edward Kelley can be taken as a starting point.

10. Our operations will be veiled in a manufactured ve-neer of politics and internal conflict. We must pretend to be royalists in the absence of a monarch. Our banners will be decorated with aristocratic imagery while we appear to be deflowered by administrative strife. Our by-laws will be so obscure that our most minor indiscretions will be escalated into acts of treason. Expulsions will be frequent and denouncements a matter of course. Our public relations will be undermined by a continual cycle of scandal and dissent.

11. The most duplicitous among us will be exalted and revered, though never in a context that exposes our doctrines. We'll cloak ourselves in misdirection and pass undetected through the ruins of Occulture. We'll openly announce the core of our beliefs, yet none will discern their true nature. They'll think us little more than pretentious obscurantists desperately seeking attention.

12. All the while, we'll carry out our real work in secret. We must spare no expense in our realization of the word of our capricious god. Our altars will be aligned with the monuments of former Yugoslavia in defiance of first principles. They'll be draped in linens of extravagance and lace which will be pilfered from the houses of the self-obsessed. We'll adorn them with fabulous candelabras that burn with pure cocaine. We'll trace our magic circles in lines of naphtha and nepenthe and circumscribe them with the names of fallen prophets—we'll honour Fantômas and Booji Boy and Mary Tyler Moore, along with Henry Darger, Raymond Roussel, Dorothy Parker, and Divine.

13. New forms of worship will naturally arise to replace the arid remains of tradition. The Neo-Decadent Occultist composes palindromes in the tongues of angels, paints them in spirals of mascara on candles made from the fat of their investors, and leaves them burning on the doorsteps of their representatives in the hour before sunrise, not to affect their political leanings, but to incite them into delicious scandals and public relations disasters.

14. We'll transcribe our catechisms onto contraband cigarettes and hyperinflationary banknotes. We'll make use of our new sacraments in elaborate rites to petition the gods of international trade. The resulting fluctuations in the value of currency will be our principal source of oracular wisdom. We'll circumambulate our Ka'aba against a swiftly-flowing river of failed banks and ruined economies, the waters ever threatening to pull us under but for the steadfastness of our faith.

15. Our adepts will resurrect the art of funerary howling and administer our services in embassies and brothels. The legions of the dead will swarm in overflowing droves through the dossiers of diplomats and their more worldly informers. Thus will we give rise to bold new forms of necromancy and a novel approach to the grimoires. Our magical pacts will be legally binding and sealed with the protocols of national security.

16. Lascivious cyphers in hexadecimal Kabbalah will be scrawled in the margins of the apocrypha; we'll craft expansion modules for electronic toys that elucidate our maxims in the language of the birds; our initials will be carved in luminiferous aether and every manner of arcana will be attributed to the letters, then we'll permute them, weigh them, transpose them, and combine them to form an alphabet of artifice and triviality. We'll pepper our canticles with preposterous lies and blatant contradictions. Only when the Akashic Record has been thoroughly falsified may our axioms be read between the lines.

17. The one thing Τὸ Μέγα Θηρίον got unquestionably right is the necessity of aspiring to the unattainable. To this end, let us bring this manifesto to a close with a litany in honour of the Absolute.

Liber Absconditum

O God, my God, you are a psalter scribed in Morse code, a clerical error in the Book of Formation, a rosary stained with diesel fuel, and a tantrum in the Tabernacle.

You are a vellum-bound volume of the most exquisite pornography in a tongue so decrepit that none can read it. Every one of your priests has been thoroughly defiled in their attempts to comprehend you.

I have sought you in the back rooms of the pleasure-houses of Pattaya where you slipped out through a servant's exit and took refuge in the night. Now you wander through the maze-like streets of the Casbah in Algiers like a diplomatic envoy in revolt against their country. None know your name, yet the most common of criminals have had you at their table. Your iconography is as irreverent as a rat in a ciborium.

Still I seek you in the Brutalist towers of Le Corbusier, in the abandoned dark rides of fallen carnivals and the glitches of bootlegged console games, in the discrepancies of an intelligentsia fallen into obsolescence, and in errata, abscondita, and navigational anomalies of all varieties.

I will never find you, yet in the course of my search I will pass into houses of ineffable splendour. I'll surreptitiously attend a clandestine séance in a hidden penthouse of the Ryugyong Hotel, stage a coup d'état from the former embassy of the Free State of Fiume, perform a midnight mass in a shipping container lost deep in the jungles of Malaysia, and spend several months scanning shortwave broadcasts in a frigid Siberian winter.

You are a pair of transposed digits in the binary code that comprises the visible world. You forever manage to elude detection while leaving your signature on every atom of space.

To pursue you is to lose you, yet to lose you is to gain the Crown.

ELECTRONIC GAMING

Arturo Calderon
Hadrian Flyte
Colby Smith

1. As officially-sanctioned online platforms will not satisfy the soul-consuming need for ludic experiences in the post-"pay-to-win" world, the Neo-Decadents will have to immerse themselves in virus-infested emulator download sites, where handheld consoles such as the Wonderswan and the Neo Geo Pocket Color can show us glimpses of a cancelled-too-soon kaleidoscopic twenty-first century entertainment experience soon to be replaced by insipid and mind-numbing mobile phone games with more advertisements than Nathan Road in Hong Kong at the turn of the century.

2. Shigeru Miyamoto—the Linnaeus of electronic gaming; not merely a descriptor of the alternative ecosystems and biologies of Nintendo games; he is also a most gracious deity, providing a cathode refuge from polluted reality, creating for the benefit and pleasure of others rather than himself. Neo-Decadent Gamers are to be

the Christian Scientists of our time, adopting the role of pixel biologists and acolytes for the informal creed of Miyamotoism. They must abandon cheat codes, Game Genies, Nintendo Power guides; the game is a petri dish and the microscope is the controller. So, too, will every button pressed be in homage to Miyamoto. When the world wilts, the road to Nirvana will be a Rainbow Road.

3. Remixing the derivé and Homo Ludens concepts for a fast-growing and aggressively absorbing capitalist era, Neo-Decadent Gamers will not surround themselves with sports simulation players waiting year after year for the same game in a new glossy package, or Neo-Fascist shooter addicts who wish they could restore their countries to their former, though historically inaccurate, glory. Instead, they will take back the notion of freedom that should have always been the goal in the digital era. Holographic rainbows running in 8k. The valley of the uncanny nothing but a distant memory in the back of a Mori Masashiro retired mind. No reward system slaves allowed, only 21st century virtual flâneurs across the multi-platform spectrum.

4. Carve ihai for the rusty corpses of arcade machines. Leave the quarters of sapphire-eyed children and dirty, chain-smoking teenagers in their dead bellies for their journey into the underworld, so the shells of their cabinets shall be weighed by the scale of Maat. Emulation is ancestor worship. No tokens, no prizes, only homage to the departed through Fatalities and Hadouken.

5. "Are you a boy or a girl?" Such an insulting Neo-Passéist question should never be asked again. With outmoded notions of identity soon to be marooned in the same mindscape now populated by monogamy, monotheism and materialism (3 big boring Ms), Neo-Decadent games will offer a wide range of alternatives for the player to customize their avatars far beyond the binary system. Gender fluidity will no longer be the exception but the rule that will open new ways of interaction, finally demolishing the chest-beating machismo and awkwardly-handled, sexually frustrated video channels that believe electronic entertainment must exclusively please the needs of white conservative man-children.

6. The Neo-Decadent Gamer no longer concerns themselves with the tangible. Direction, balance, and perception are withering senses in a sea of digital supplication. It is imperative that the Neo-Decadent Gamer cease relying on external stimuli and instead seek to reconstruct themselves in code. The Idoru are the new reality, the champions of an idealized existence beyond the self and its banal reliance on permanence.

7. The electronic game presents itself as the greatest possibility to realize *Gesamtkunstwerk*. The Neo-Decadent Gamer should not only be a consumer but a creator, a priest and a god at once. Pushing the limits of their imaginations and technical prowess, the Neo-Decadent Gamer will create games on the scale of creation myths, Wagnerian operas, scientific paradigm shifts.

8. Linearity is death. Power is now abstract, illicit, and diaphanous, with no reward beyond the gamer's inevitable degradation. The Neo-Decadent Gamer no longer merely "plays" a game or a role within a cybernated construct but surrenders to the eradication of self. Resonance replaces perception and installs its own direction, consuming the player in the process. Where linearity stifles the soul, the cubiform supplants it.

9. Environment as character, removed from the predictable plight of a protagonist. The Neo-Decadent Gamer seeps between intention and setting, uprooting logarithmic trees and mining each artifacted rock. Only destruction and inevitable resurrection can distil the essence of time these transcended gamers ingurgitate to see beyond the plight of the constructed man. Corruption and renewal are dalliances.

10. We reject the oppressive conformity of Westernization. Games are capable of the same cultural transference as literature but are rarely given the chance in the race to stripmine ingenuity to serve the colourless imaginations of the Anglosphere. To play games in a Neo-Decadent reality is to stumble helplessly through the unknown until it fuses with our skin, consuming us in biotropic bliss. Language is the new mycelium and we long to enter that eternal mycorrhiza.

11. Electronic games must get rid of goals, time-wasting soul-numbing trophies that reward gamers for sticking

to obsolete parameters which do not let them explore every inch of the virtual worlds to which they have access. Brand new concepts and outside-the-box approaches to gameplay must not only be encouraged but demanded from every developer and designer. An offspring of *LSD Simulator* and *Yume Nikki* without the unpleasant feeling of dread after every step. A *GTA*-inspired sandbox game without the gangster lifestyle escapism, just a vast area where you can roam free, from hospitals to school, from canyons to outer space and all the points in between. Burning Gothic cathedrals where a magical girl can attain Nirvana with the help of a César Vallejo-quoting non-playable character. The centre of the Big Bang itself from the perspective of a newborn black hole. The console as a Japanese-developed, Chinese-manufactured, American-imported TARDIS that can be a golden key for our inner doors of perception, a mind-altering drug for straight-edgers, or just a glorified paperweight that will eventually download the newest version of a boring and dull franchise perpetuating itself through time. A Neo-Decadent knows how to choose wisely.

12. As a total abandonment of the industry-imposed, controlled-movement methods inside the digital oneiric architecture of electronic gaming, most people have developed their own way of avoiding the tedious task of simply going from point A to B and get rid of the almost coitus interruptus conclusions from what must be a more kaleidoscopic experience. The same way memorizing and studying close-to-your-heart verses from a long-form Modernist poem can lead to the revelation

of savoury secrets hidden between lines, spending long insomnia-ridden nights can reveal wormholes waiting for you behind portraits in a polygonal Mushroom Kingdom, or that the combination of blue-and-orange portals can guide you through retro-futuristic edge lands while running away from an egomaniacal AI in less time than necessary to decide which would be the best outfit for hitting the arcades. Breaking the unbreakable and seeing the invisible should be spiritual dogmas for the Neo-Decadent Gamer. A third-eye opening approach to a 48-hour-long RPG where instead of facing an eldritch abomination in an existential duel with the fate of entire galaxies at stake, you decide to go on a pleasant side quest in order to grow radishes and cabbages, the freshest and most delicious vegetables that those 32-bit High Fantasy worlds have ever seen. As fast as a Bugatti Chiron Super Sport 300 or as slow as a three-toed sloth, there is no goal to stick to except for the absolute pursuit of jouissance.

13. The ludic impulse was never to be taken as a middle-aged White Dad distraction but as an alchemic desire for knowledge. The urge to take apart your cartridges to see what is inside, blowing into them up to the point of irreversibly damaging their limited-storage chips in order to make this once-state-of-the-art technology work properly. Beautifully Chaotic results of altermodern rituals. Neo-Decadent gaming understood as magick. Your grimoires are the dust-covered video games guides, where maps, glitches, combos and passwords are listed for you to recite in a darkened room, only lit by the candles' reflection on a collage made by fragments of limited-edi-

tion PS1 discs on your own altar. Attaining a soul-immersing state so deep you can play whole titles without the need of a console. The ecstatic delight of the sight of a digital sigil in the back of a room inside the memory of a summer afternoon in the company of a long-forgotten system. A software never to become obsolete and with an unlimited number of levels for an adventurous spirit to explore as long as there are electronic heart containers on your health bar.

14. Tournaments! The gamers' Grecian Olympics, their gladiator shows, their jousting matches! But lo! manipulating their thumbs with the speed and grace of a spider weaving its web, they play their games in public (not for themselves but) for the corrosive potion Mountain Dew; the golden, savoury, powdery image of Doritos, upon beholding fingers licked in reflex; the iron-fisted, nihilistic multinational corporation that creates these games from nothing (more miraculous than abiogenesis!) but sees no art in them, sees no respect for developers under their tattered wings—crushing dreams, financial security, and dignity with a gesture of the hand, a squint of the eye, a shift of the brow. Gamers, those adored yet despised, are no better in this state than the child seduced by Mick Maus, the revolutionary (like a bull set for a matador to sink his sabre into) enraptured by the colour red, the bright high school graduate dreaming their dreams vicariously through deans—drunk with the blood of Caesars—overseeing for-profit universities. Thus, the Neo-Decadent Gamer resists this, holding tournaments on behalf of nobody but themselves. They rig abandoned

warehouses with fresh electricity and televisions and squat for weeks on end with the sounds of FPS and fighters resounding for miles while the police are too frightened to shut it down, taking the finest drugs on downtime to jack up their game and find God through pixels and 3D models, holding Bacchic orgies regardless of whether the rookie or the veteran is the victor of a match.

15. The Neo-Decadent Gamer forms harems outside the game and marriages within the game. A Queen Elizabeth in the gameworld, a Genghis Khan in the waking world.

INTERPERSONAL RELATIONSHIPS

Justin Isis

The Paucity of Relationships

Friends and lovers, parents and children, husbands and wives, husbands and husbands, wives and wives, employers and employees, teachers and students, masters and servants: we have witnessed them all, and all of them bore us.

Almost all artforms have seen increased specialization, increased renovation of generic conventions over time—except interpersonal relationships. Technology soars ahead, but our repertoire of human connections remains curiously, almost medievally limited. We satisfy ourselves with surface agitations, trivial variations. Much has been made of the recent generation-wide transition away from monogamy and stifling domestic and familial bonds, but conceptually, little has changed. Minor reconfigurations are taken for revolutions, while the dull heart of convention thuds away, rarely varying its rhythm.

"This is my partner, Jude."
"This is my friend, Gottfried."
"This is my mother, Stacy."

Beneath these confident assertions lie tired old bones with thin modern skins, and in practice, most interpersonal relationships devolve into predictable patterns and routines. These conditions are reasonable for a primitive race struggling to make sense of itself: less appropriate for a modern technological civilization with advanced aspirations. In concert with our ongoing reformulation of every aspect of human existence, we, the Neo-Decadents, intend to expand the range and possibilities of relationships, bringing them in line with our novel sensibilities.

Transcending Transaction

We classify transactional relationships as those that can be readily reduced to:

1. An agreed-upon exchange, monetary or otherwise, usually mediated by symbolic vocalizations (talking).

Example: Yevgeny is a capitalist. He employs Bruno to remove the feces deposited by youthful vandals from the doorstep of his wig shop. In exchange, Bruno receives a handful of vouchers.

Example: Ziggy is Ian's liege lord. Ziggy is placed above Ian in the political hierarchy, and he eats the freeze dried noodles they have salvaged from the dumpster before Ian does.

2. The symbolic gilding of a physiological process or means of survival (procreation, mutual defence, the retrieval of resources).

Example: Muhammad is a male. He regularly has detailed oral sex with his "wife," Carly.

Example: Carly has given birth to Gustave. Gustave relies on her for food and shelter. Gustave frequently makes curt, stereotyped vocalizations pertaining to the presence or absence of his "mother."

In these examples, we are deep in the realm of automatic associations in which little that could properly be called human is present. We might in fact call these elaborated reflexes rather than relationships as such, given that all of them have clear analogues in other species. Neither can the emotions associated with them be called specifically human: it makes as much sense to speak of loyal bees, affectionate rats, cooperative wolves and compassionate crows. The tortuously-labelled (d)alliances and distractions of our urban artist-scientists are built on foundations of gross utility.

But NATURE and NECESSITY shall play no role in our experimental relationships.

Silence: The Renovation of Symbolic Vocabulary

We have already mentioned the appalling complacency of those ready at any time to announce the existence of their friends, partners, parents, etc. In practice, very little is ever done with these friends and partners and parents that does not consist of parroted vocalizations uttered with the aim of reaching a predetermined consensus. This parade of pleasantries ushers them through life, until they are quite dead without ever having done or noticed anything. Worse, the simple delectation of modern conveniences is frequently interrupted, distracting from immediate sensory experience:

"I'm wondering what to do with my life."
"Sonic Youth released many interesting albums with different styles."
"I don't appreciate the way you've been ignoring me recently."
"I'm worried about the destruction of the environment and the end of the world."
"What are your plans for the weekend?"

When performing basic functions such as resting, eating, bathing, and smoking, there is no need for the proliferation of meaningless statements and questions, which are almost always repetitions of received ideas or demands for narcotic reassurance and "solidarity," rather than spurs to any concrete, constructive or exploratory action.

The assumption that vocalizations ("verbal communication") must undergird all significant relationships is one of the most limiting falsehoods to have been inflicted on the populace. Beyond their basic transactional function of coordinating activities, vocalizations usually accomplish little of any importance. Worse, the habit inevitably leads to senile repetition, as stories and opinions calcify over decades. Each person begins by surprising themselves with their own words and ends up enslaved to the tired collection of routines to which they have reduced themselves. Each speaker becomes both spider and fly, wrapping themselves in numbing strands of language. This dreadful self-mummification is encouraged by all sectors of society.

Most people feel uncomfortable spending long periods around others without exchanging vocalizations. The compulsive need to "break the silence" is proof of how well we have been trained to lull each other with chatter. We are encouraged to repeat the appropriate second or third-hand opinions and sell each other on the merits of the latest corporate entertainments: this is known as "staying current" or "keeping up with the conversation." But nothing could be less novel or current than the ritual reinforcement of these same tired patterns.

Deprived of recourse to verbal cliches, humans become aware once more of their physical existence, and of the irreducible reality of other people. Novel relationships, then, demand hygienic silence as a spur to the development and exploration of genuine sympathy.

A simple exercise. Take two humans who are tentatively interested in each other and force them to spend several hours together without speaking. They should be discouraged, also, from passive spectation of media productions. If at an initial loss for what to "do," we recommend simple shared activities: running, dancing, cooking, drawing. But the point is to do "nothing" together, or in other words, to discover activities which are not normally considered activities at all—rather than discussing "interests," the particulars of respective "backgrounds," naive fantasies of the future, or any other tenuous self-conceptions.

Whenever possible, vocalization should be replaced with action. Before meeting, those seeking to establish a relationship should decide on the premises governing their interactions: a constellation or juxtaposition of activities to be devised together in advance (or generated randomly). Such a constellation might be:

1. Glum cereal.
2. Kali bhakti.
3. Core work.
4. Portraiture.
5. Minor indecency.

Kwame and Haruka meet in a public park. After examining their list of assigned activities, they flip a coin to determine who will do what. After the toss, Kwame focuses on the even tasks while Haruka addresses the odds. While Haruka morosely eats a bowl of Frosted Flakes, Kwame attains the primal gnosis of Time, the Black Goddess. Haruka performs exercises designed to strengthen her core muscles, while Kwame completes an oil painting of her in action. Finally Haruka confronts a passing child and coughs in its face before making an insulting gesture. Unable to verbally discuss what has just occurred, the two are left to embody it with their proximity. Later, as they embrace, both imagine a tigress tearing open a young girl's taut abdomen.

By means of a constantly improvised and evolving symbolic vocabulary, emotions and "personal connections" will be achieved outside of the easy stream of cliches, and human sentiment will slip free of the commodified slave roles we have been taught to inhabit since birth.

Private Languages

Once some mastery of silence is achieved, participants can resume vocalization, albeit with a new purpose: the construction of a private language. The aim here is not only to avoid the limiting premises inherent in familiar phrases and methods of address, but to produce entirely new categories of experience.

Given that our habitual distinction between "internal" states and outward occurrences is largely a matter of convention, the replacement of second-hand language with a new, collaborative, private vocabulary will allow for greater intimacy: not only new events but new object-categories will rise into perceptibility.

Gaurav and Marilena meet in the forest at night, having established an hlemetic abdomance over the course of several months. They clear a space in the grass and trace the shining figure of a tescalymn. Gaurav recites the mayamotic satechrism, and Marilena assumes a leolithic posture. Carneal keenings and marnorations ensue.

The discussion turns to technical matters: proper methods of graling, how to angle an aplanaromic latapulce; whether a yuriobastic diogromal is necessary to confirm the presence of a hovering zolvrus, or if a crescexular hapaxylomat is better suited to the task: assorted digressions in the cataquirial mode. With wumulous and increasingly garbid gestures, they refine their iphimenial strategies. Before long things have progressed to phettic salvery and heated valampering.

Gaurav has brought along a basket of priscal mogic; Marilena presents her furry drendel for stroking. They observe vouls, tharns, a coricated ryx, and the delights of a serrete oromb in the middle distance, encloured with thinial shading. Marilena shivens like an oplerole, and Gaurav captures the entraiture of her face, its slow pluvulations. They maneuver each other into the air's halaphonal craizure and produce a great gloptic chirk, a furtive melovial prake and the final shared rush of gloamy locean. The night sky tarters down to the treetops in an overwhelming thaliasm.

Common Phrases as Emotional Vessels

If participants struggle at first to convey their desires and emotions without the use of conventional vocalizations, they should simply use whatever phrases are at hand, *provided that their literal meaning is unconnected with what they intend to express.* In other words, they should focus on imparting their meaning through tone and delivery, making use of random phrases (either generated manually, or provided by an app or other automatic method). Whenever possible, personal pronouns should be omitted, and references to current events, topical figures, fads, scandals, etc. should be avoided.

Gertrude and Spud enjoy sharing various emotions. One day, Gertrude returns home feeling drained from a heated theological argument at the stray dog shelter. In desperation, she throws herself at Spud's feet and checks her smartphone for phrasal content. Her cracked voice conveys her inner vastation as she intones one of the following:

"Springtime is the best time for drinking coffee."
"Fuzzy baseballs are like snails: there's always a sticky cherry on top."
"Sonic Youth had a limited number of ideas."

Spud, immediately taking her meaning, pours Gertrude a glass of Cabernet Sauvignon and buys her a corn dog from the corner store. Meat, mustard, fried batter and good red wine soon assuage Gertrude's frayed nerves and shaken convictions.

"Pluto and Eris are cold, dead, trans-Neptunian objects," Spud remarks.

The two smile, remove their socks and walk barefoot over the hardwood floor.

Experimental Relationships

Over time, both the taxonomy of relationships and the scope of their individual intricacies will expand beyond what anyone has previously imagined. The following is in no way an exhaustive enumeration, only a brief listing of avenues for further research. It should be noted that all of the following can be attempted simultaneously, and aside from certain exceptions, none of them have a fixed number of participants: each is equally viable as a dyad, triad, tetrad, etc. The overlapping of relationships should eventually attain an almost orchestral quality (given that no one occupies a single role for anyone else, something like this already prevails, albeit in a vastly more limited form than the one we aim to achieve).

Director/Actor

Whenever they encounter each other, the director explains the actor's motivations and provides suggestions on how they can improve whatever they happen to be doing at the time. The actor feels compelled to acquiesce, even when the director's suggestions seem to have little bearing on their present circumstances.

Zachariah has gone to a nightclub to immerse himself in the physicality of teenagers. His highly technical dancing attracts the attention of Brian, and the two adjourn to the bar for light conversation. Just then Zachariah's director, Omar, interrupts them:

"You weren't really performing those dance moves correctly . . . you didn't seem to be feeling it. Now with this conversation you're getting a bit overwrought. Let's restage the past ten minutes but with more fluidity and casual princeliness."

Zachariah concedes the relevance of Omar's commentary and reperforms his actions of the past ten minutes. Brian is impressed with his commitment, and agrees that this second take is superior to the first. Their conversation is repeated, then resumes where it left off. Omar smiles with satisfaction.

Laughing Units

The goal is to induce laughter in the other party, without resorting to obvious means. One participant may begin by laughing at a spontaneous occurrence, or interrupting a standard conversation with exaggerated contortions. Extreme levity should be maintained, even in the presence of others with whom participants share different types of relationships.

Through long association, Wilhelmina and Becky have learned to do little else but laugh maniacally whenever they encounter each other. One day, Wilhelmina notices Becky leaving the train station. Already exhausted from managing a highly taxing political campaign, Wilhelmina thinks to escape without attracting Becky's attention. But Becky quickly notices her and rushes over. Taking in Wilhelmina's haggard appearance, Becky removes her military beret and pours a small bottle of orange juice over it. Soon Wilhelmina is laughing so hard that she genuinely suffers.

Moral Arbiter/Control Group

After completing an analysis of prevailing trends, the arbiter works out a moral and ethical program derived from currently fashionable values, which is then installed in the control group. This allows the arbiter to burnish their reputation while relieving the control group of the burden of developing their own values, in effect out-sourcing their personal development.

Charles and Lawrence live together and often meet Xiaofan, who enjoys grocery shopping and imposing moral programs on others. The three are popular at social gatherings, where Charles and Lawrence frolic in a state of merry gormlessness, while Xiaofan receives approbation for his fastidious tutelage.

One day it comes to Xiaofan's attention that Charles has been poaching condiments from children at the mall:

"Hand over your ketchup packets, you delayed abortions."

While not strictly criminal, his actions are far from ethical, and are liable to expose him to comment from the more enlightened members of his social set. Worse, Charles seems to feel little remorse. Xiaofan advises him to prepare the correct requisition documents for the next time he itches to squirrel away sauces. Then he tweaks the zealousness of Charles's convictions so that he feels an appropriate regret.

Later, examining his surveillance footage, Xiaofan notices that Lawrence has been taking improper care of his potted geraniums. He swiftly sends a text message:

"It's not correct to water those plants with mouse blood. Please reflect on your actions."

After throwing the geraniums in the trash, Lawrence consults a sage to learn more suitable ways to dispose of his surplus mice.

It should be noted that the arbiter is not required to personally adopt any morals they assign to others, and to expect them to do so shows a misunderstanding of this relationship.

The Aged Herald

A relationship relying on an age disparity. In public, the aged herald announces the imminent arrival of their younger associate, whether the associate is likely to arrive or not. In the event that the associate arrives, the herald explains in greater detail what activities the associate is likely to perform (if others are present) or remains silent (if there is no one else around).

A group of pearl divers has convened in a Moroccan restaurant. Supporting himself with a cane, Edmund makes his way over to their table and addresses those present in a loud and resonant voice:

"Luigi is going to be here any minute now. You're not at all ready for what he's got planned. He's been working on this for months. Nothing can prepare you for what he's got up his sleeve, so to speak. It won't be pretty but it will be necessary. I don't want anyone to move until he gets here. Not even to go to the bathroom. Just sit tight and keep your hands folded. You really can't imagine what is about to happen."

Eventually Luigi arrives, to the great excitement and trepidation of the table. Luigi apologizes for being somewhat overhyped, and the table, remembering similar experiences with their own heralds, buys him several strong drinks.

Executioner/Victim

The executioner kills the victim.

This need not be accomplished literally—a symbolic enactment is sufficient (burning or defacing an image immediately before, during, or after a natural death). Regardless of how it occurs, the executioner takes full responsibility for the victim's demise.

Nadezhda notices that a one year old girl has been following her for some time. The young child eventually crawls into a business meeting at the investment bank where Nadezdha works. Things become tense, until all present realize with a laugh that the small girl is simply an executioner.

"That's Maxine, she's my murderer. Doesn't look like much, does she? Still, guess my life is in her hands..."

The executioner shoulders an enormous responsibility, that of an entire human life. When in proximity to their victim or engaged in conversation with them, the executioner should maintain concentration on an imagined interval in which the victim will pass from a "living" to a "non-living" state (the frequent difficulty of pinpointing an exact moment is part of the exercise). Similarly, the executioner's mere presence will induce thoughts of death in the victim, spurring both to more timely completion of projects and more desperate involvement in life.

Precursor/Revivalist

The precursor prepares a detailed diary record of their activities each day. After reading it, the revivalist attempts to recreate the precursor's routines, interactions and consumption choices the following day—visiting the same places, eating the same foods, even, when possible, carrying on the same conversations with the same people. Any deviations (usually resulting from uncontrollable factors) should be treated as extremely significant, and possible portents of future events in the precursor's own life.

Elias has been doing his best to re-enact each day described in Santiago's diary. During their usual morning meeting, Elias recounts his successes and failures:

"Your girlfriend was a little surprised to see me, but she was extremely gracious about letting me stay over. Said she couldn't really tell the difference between us. In a good way, of course. Not much happened at your father's funeral though. . .I mean, I was the only one there. So I had to improvise a bit. And tuna on rye for lunch was definitely the right choice."

The revivalist experiences the peace that results from never having to think of what to do next, while the precursor enjoys the luxury of knowing that their seemingly trivial decisions will affect the entirety of someone else's existence.

Transmitter/Receiver

The transmitter concentrates on relaying mental impressions to objects generally considered to be non-sentient, extending even to natural landscape features (cliffs, mountains, rivers). Anyone coming into contact with the receivers created in this fashion must examine any moods and feelings evoked.

Colby has returned home to find Felix puttering around in the kitchen:

"Getting some interesting vibes from this microwave oven. Filioque controversy. . .baklava. . .Hagia Sophia. Aversive, intolerant energy."

"Close. I charged it with Dracula scenes last night. Vlad the Impaler. . .it's become surly and anti-Turkish."

Non-human animals may also function as transmitters and receivers, in whatever conjunctions are deemed appropriate.

Vandal/Property

The vandal makes alterations to the property's appearance by providing them with new articles of clothing, giving them unexpected haircuts, or altering their wardrobe in accordance with passing whims and inspirations: drawing or painting over their clothes, ornamenting them with flowers, cutting holes in their pants, etc.

Despite the implications of their title, the vandal takes responsibility for the property's appearance, with an eye to rendering it more timely in ways the property would not have anticipated.

Theodora becomes troubled by Quentin's bare shoulder and applies a temporary tattoo of a silver salamander. Later, when Quentin is drinking tea, she cuts off a piece of his hat.

"Mid-September now, yeah? Can't have an intact hat. Here's some celery—you know what to do with it."

The "stylist" label is not strictly appropriate here, since the vandal does to an extent actively work to sabotage the property's appearance, although always with an eye to adding spontaneous contrasts, interrupting any bland sartorial harmonies with riotous invention and unexpected novelty. Any inconvenience generated is offset by the reactions provoked in observers.

Platonic Enemies

Most people acquire enemies haphazardly—if they acquire them at all. Petty antipathies result in grudges, which are often barely sustained past the initial infatuation or bloom of negative passion. With the abolition of public duels, we have lost not only the necessity of taking our convictions and actions seriously (lest there be immediate mortal consequences), but any real conception of enmity itself. As a result, we muddle about, secretly trying to defeat ourselves, or else fixate on perceived foes who are usually little more than fantasy figures (televised phantoms of politicians and celebrities). Fad philosophies of mindfulness and non-attachment starve our honest antagonism to a miserable, childish spite.

Ideal enmity, consisting of the imposition of strict limits and the long-lasting maintenance of concern for another person, is one of the strongest interpersonal relationships. Enemies should be assigned to each other at birth and should sustain the relationship for several decades at the minimum (a formal exchange of enmity rings may be completed in young adulthood to signify the union). Severe penalties, such as the amputation of a toe or finger, should be imposed for breaking enmity. To permanently opt out of the relationship, a severance ceremony should be staged, in which the party seeking to leave should admit their personal failings.

Without necessarily exceeding the bounds of the law, platonic enemies should be expected to discourage each other in all things, which will, of course, require regular monitoring of each other's activities. News of misfortune must be greeted with triumph.

Ramon has heard that his enemy, Susan, has become mortally ill. Aware that Susan has been working multiple jobs to support her three children as a single mother, Ramon sends her a handwritten letter:

"Congratulations on the lung cancer, Susan. I await your death with great eagerness. Little time remains to you—which I'm sure you'll waste."

After being fired from his job at the semiconductor factory, Félicien has rapidly exhausted his savings. His wife, Lola, has left him. Despondent and alone, he receives a call from his enemy, Jennifer:

"Once again you've dug your own grave. You can't even take care of yourself. . .you don't deserve to be loved. You're getting exactly what you deserve."

This arrangement will abolish loneliness forever.

Post-Naturalist Relationships in the Aeon of Possibility

The examples given, while only sketches, are sufficient to suggest the nature of the relationships we intend to explore. The role of ever-advancing technology in mediating and facilitating these novel connections has barely been mentioned, but it is enough to stress its critical importance. If we have underplayed it somewhat, it is only because almost everyone takes technological progress for granted, whereas common conceptions of interpersonal bonds are at least five hundred years out of date. Until now little has been expected, but much must be demanded if we are to achieve anything.

It is no longer permissible to allow laziness and atavism to prevail. Our options have been limited to stale configurations and obsolete roles, but now an expanded repertoire of relationships awaits us, should we have the courage to embrace it. In defiance of boredom and acting always with the rigour of scientists and the good humour of grave robbers exhuming neglected tombs of primitive sentiment, we, the Neo-Decadents, proclaim a new program of experimental relationships: we, who would entangle ourselves with each other, dancing, merging, forming social shapes as fantastic as fire ant rafts and dissolving them as soon as our aims are accomplished. Where there has been only convention, we will achieve humanity.

ENGLISH POETRY

Jeremy Reed

Neo-Decadence as the New Real

To me, Decadence represents the future and the new real, rather than the historic module of an objectively observable social degeneration in which the arts are implicated by the etiolation of a corrupt aesthetic. In my creative application of the genre, Decadence is renewable as oxygen; it's always ahead, in the way that imagination is the fastest route of perceptual travel in the brain's complex organisations, as the subjective expression of consciousness.

While one could argue that Wilde's *The Picture of Dorian Gray* was historically the epitome of decadence, it was also the first British underground novel, in that it subverted normative sex, deviated from conventional morality and introduced opium as a smacked-out recreational drug into the remit of fiction. That the novel's influence became at the time of his trial a scandal, and its homoerotic themes suppressed, meant that it was only picked up on much later in prototypical gay novels like Andrew Holleran's *The Dancer From The Dance* (1978), and Edmund White's *Nocturnes For The King of Naples* (1978), in which the sort of saturated imagery at which Wilde excelled, accessorises the narrative, not as artifice, but as a multisensory unit of abandonment to anonymous sex; as an altogether newer and realer paradigm than its straight equivalents.

My introduction to Neo-Decadent writing came about through reading the post-apocalyptic novels of JG Ballard and William Burroughs, pioneering futurists who totally re-modified consensus reality not only into dystopian modernity, but as a visionary overview of the incorporation of high-tech into the psychological, social and environmental developments of what Ballard called the visionary present. And both writers concerned themselves not with object travel to sci-fi localities, but with locating those potentialities in the domains of inner space, in itself the continuously updated resource of Neo-Decadence. In Ballard's technocratic novel *Crash* (1973), symphorophilia and car crash fetishism align the body's sexuality with cabin ergonomics and automotive devices that become the sexual object itself, and the novel's protagonist Vaughan, fixated on car crash injuries, is a pathological crash voyeur finding in the geometry of wounds the imperials of erotic stimulus. Ballard's mapping of a new diagrammatic sexualised body exploited not only for its beauty, but for its injuries, presented mechanophilia as normal, and in doing so became paradigmatic of what was to become cyberpunk, with its conversion of the analogue body into digital.

During the seventies, when Ballard wrote a stream of techno-visionary novels—*The Atrocity Exhibition* (1970), *Crash* (1973), *Concrete Island* (1974), and *High Rise* (1975); highly transgressive works in which idealised British middle-class gated communities were presented as the carriers of deviant psychopathologies—the word Decadent was never applied to their mediated excesses, or the lives of his affluent professionals turned potential psychopaths. The critical definition of Decadence was still polarised to *fin de siècle* anomie, so that the word was never applied to Ballard's deviated fictions in which the personal also becomes a product. What other novelist, as instanced in *High Rise*, would risk opening a novel with its protagonist in the process of eating the hindquarters of his pet dog:

'Later, as he sat on his balcony eating the dog, Dr Robert Laing reflected on the unusual events that had taken place within this huge apartment building during the previous three months.'

The deliberately understated term 'unusual events' refers within the novel to social anarchy within the complex, aimed at undermining a hierarchy in which the privileged occupy the building's upper floors, (i.e. a professional elite), while the poorer tenants occupy the lower; the conflict in process disables the building's amenities and services, aiming systematically at wrecking and looting apartments. When the escalating carnage subsides, with the swimming pool stuffed with dismembered bodies, Laing feels the superiority not only of survival, but of having taken on the role of morphine-addicted avatar to the building's devastated survivors:

'Dusk had settled, and the embers of the fire glowed in the darkness. The silhouette of the large dog on the spit resembled the flying figure of a mutilated man, soaring with immense energy across the night sky, embers glowing with the fire of jewels in his skin.'

The concept of eating roast dog by a member of the medical profession, not only as an abnormal experience, but as a pointer to the decay in society's ethical and moral traditions, is a supreme moment of Neo-Decadence situated in the cosmic futurism that Ballard's novels inhabit. And over my long period of friendship and correspondence with Ballard, he insisted always that sci-fi inhabited the wrong space, and that it was the limitless frontiers of inner, not outer, space that best accommodated near futures and end times rather than the proposed colonisation of the galaxy through interplanetary travel.

Ballard's fiction as an indication of sub-scenes with an insider's code to placing tomorrow before today, occupies no categorizable genre, except the eponymous term Ballardian. His novels explore the collapse of the distinction between vision and madness, most often in the socially acceptable as carriers of the potentially emergent psychopath. His visionary subversion of cultural forms in fiction arguably finds its interface in synthetic biology that attempts to redesign organisms for useful purposes by engineering them to have new abilities. Ballard re-treated fiction, having briefly trained in medicine, as a biomedical module that could incorporate near-future technologies, in the same way that synthetic biology seeks to create new biological parts, devices and systems, or to redesign systems already present in nature. Genetic engineering in the modification of an organism's genome through biotechnology could appropriately be assigned a Neo-Decadent context within science, little different in its textual applications to how Huysmans, the author of the seminally decadent *Against Nature* (1884), plays with altered states through the introduction of synaesthesia. The two occupy a similar resonance, separate in time, but ultimately not so different in their design to re-edit the body's capacity to experience the new real through enhanced cellular discourse.

What I'm proposing is that Ballard's novels from the period 1970-1983, not only reinvent the body as coefficient of weirdness, nowhere better exemplified than in the condensed fictions of *The Atrocity Exhibition* (1970), and *Crash* (1973), but integrate the practices of synthetic biology into their subjects' psychological and physical makeup.

It was William S. Burroughs who in *Naked Lunch* declared 'Western man is externalizing himself in the form of gadgets,' and there's a strong case for arguing that Burroughs is not only the precursor of cyberpunk, but through his immersion in drug subcultures and their corresponding depravities, the originator of psychoactive politics, in itself a form of retribalized Decadence subverting fixed notions of consensus reality. That non-ordinary experience should be the active ingredient to writing that pushes out psychic frontiers, and that altered perception of the small strangenesses surrounding us, our best possible clues to reality, is seminal to writing forward rather than backward as the vehicle adopted by mainstream convention.

Baudelaire, as the originator of Decadence, took pride in his rejection by bourgeois society, and in identifying poetry with criminality, in the same way that Burroughs the habituated junky wrote precisely from an outlaw's viewpoint in his lifelong violation of the morality, politics and drug-prohibitions of modern America. That drugs, by opening pathways to altered or alternative realities in the user's consciousness, threaten to undermine the accepted scientific view of physical reality, and are criminalised as a consequence, categorizes them, and particularly hallucinogens, as potentially disruptive of ideologies dependent on perspective realism to maintain the social order. We could argue equally that Baudelaire's is a very minor strain of Decadence compared to Burroughs' belief that language is a virus from outer space. As a prototypical cyberpunk, Burroughs epitomises those aspects of Decadence that seem an inherited gene of lowlife in collision with high tech.

Although *Naked Lunch* was scrambled together in the late fifties, Burroughs' evocation of corporeal decay and cannibalism could equally belong to Huysmans' or Baudelaire's revulsion of the body as ultimately putrescent entropy. What brings Burroughs ahead of his generation, and aligns him like Ballard with synthetic biology, is the nonlinear cut-up style used as a disruptive methodology. And because of its essentially random or mechanical basis for text generation, combined with the method of mixing text written by other writers, Burroughs' lexical mixology deemphasises the role of the writer as singular owner of his work, while simultaneously demanding of the writer that he act as judicious editor. Burroughs treats the novel in the way a mixologist prepares a cocktail of edited ingredients, like a gin or martini collage.

If the Neo-Decadent emphasis from Ballard and Burroughs onwards was on the meta-biological, meta-chemical and synthetic psychological concepts replacing the themes of social realism in the mainstream novel, and the utopian tendencies of earlier science fiction, then its inheritor was William Gibson, arguably the progenitor of cyberpunk. Gibson's combination in *Neuromancer* (1984) of punk attitudes applied to high technologies featuring AI and cybernetics, created in the process the sort of private time systems and space-times that characterise his unabatingly futuristic novels in which the realities he describes are already events in the future. And to me, Gibson, like Ballard, is essentially a poet, his meticulously detailed imagery and his highly condensed chapters reading more like fragments of an epic poem than preconceived models of organised fiction.

Do we view Neo-Decadence then, as a technocultural bacteriology, an inherited sensibility individualised into its expansion, or as a subjective phenomenon launched in opposition to the ethical and moral restrictions imposed by society's scientific methodologies and modelling practices?

To me, it's about the individual or type being sucked forward into ultimate novelty by the forces of imagination that shape the new real into its appropriately expansive psychic postcode. Both in my own practice and in my reading, writing is only outstanding to me through the quality and originality of its imagery; as stripped of the image it remains nothing but words and ideas, like a non-alcoholic drink. And the image is a right-brain involuntary experience, the right hemisphere predominating in perceptual, holistic, manipulo-spatial and gestalt formations. Intensified visual imagery is not only seminal to Neo-Decadent writing as neural information, but also in its appeal to all the senses as the unit of behaviour or experience imagined. And this is what has always distinguished Decadent and Neo-Decadent writing from Baudelaire to Gibson, the vehicle of kinetic imagery as the equivalent of timeframes that are unforgettably filmic. I simply can't read in the absence of imagery; strings of words don't interest me. The image isn't an accessory, it's the heartbeat of compelling poetry or fiction—it's the impromptu gestalt that makes it all happen.

What Neo-Decadence provides, or should do, is the narrowing of the bandwidth between fiction and poetry, in that I've described the likes of Ballard, Burroughs and Gibson as arguably writing poetry in the more expansive space provided by prose, in a form I call meta-poetry, which reduces most other contemporary poetry to the status of employing a bleached language devoid of high-tech or the experimental unpacking of bizarre phenomenology. British poetry, unlike American, is irrevocably sucked backwards into maintaining an increasingly tired language that excludes in most cases our dizzying acceleration into techno-apocalyptic realities. I would argue that William Gibson's most recent novels, *The Peripheral* and *Agency,* are the great modern poems of our fractured times, combining Neo-Decadent tintings with visionary access to how the contemporary moment finds its place in the unsettling emergent future. My own poetry forms part of that metabolic arc that attempts to go places other poets don't dare, not only as a diagnostic of the future, but as the elevation of the ordinary through Neo-Decadent applications. Poetry least invites those who move out in front of experience, rather than take refuge behind it, but that's always been my place, going forward and still counting.

AMERICAN POETRY

Paul Cunningham

For Joyelle McSweeney

This manifesto of New Decadence is indebted to Joyelle McSweeney's 2013 Montevidayo blog post—"We Must Be Decadent, Again."

"[. . .] Everything is burning. Man's default mode is cruelty and exploitation, outrageous depredation and deprivation. We have to go backwards to find an art form that does not hide this truth under ideologies of progress or purity. The TED-talkathon, which infects every part of our political and cultural environs, amounts to a new Victorianism, the imperialistic export of progress. We must be Decadent again."

♎

We are sick.
Therefore, we make Art.

We would be sick whether the COVID-19 pandemic happened or not.

Ω

"What is the sign of every literary decadence? That life no longer dwells in the whole" [...] "The whole no longer lives at all: it is composite, calculated, artificial, an artifact."

Building off of Nietzsche's 1888 essay, "The Case of Wagner: a Musician's Problem," Regenia Gagnier has made Decadence a project of "progress": "Progress was decadent because increasing individuation led to the disintegration of the whole. In similar formulations, moral character, as the alignment of individual development with the goals of the state (what we now call governmentality) was precisely what Bohemians—both soft Bohemians such as Bloomsbury and hard Bohemians such as Verlaine or Jarry—resisted."

Ω

Anne Friedberg: "The mall is a contemporary phantasmagoria, enforcing a blindness to a range of urban blights—the homeless, beggars, crime, traffic, even weather."

Ω

The dying mall of our day is the perfect metaphor for the sick whole Gagnier focuses on. In terms of Neo-Decadence or New Decadence, the dead or dying mall should be a place of worship.

℔

In his diary, *Poetry Against All*, Johannes Göransson writes, "I read poetry for the ruins . . ."

℔

"But now the future's a part of the present." This is what the guide says when he and his group reach the toxic, radioactive belly of the Zone in Andrei Tarkovsky's *Stalker* (1979). The same Zone (aka Tallinn, Estonia) that most likely gave Tarkovsky the cancer that would kill him in 1986.

Göransson continues: "I read poetry for the ruins because they reminded me of *Stalker*, where the guide brings customers into the Zone, which may be the area infected by a toxic disaster or may be the Zone of Art, where every desire can come true. [...] Art affects the body like cancer. Home is where your heart is, homesick is what your heart is. What evil it is to be so saturated by art's strangeness."

Now, in quarantine, our only future is the present. *"Decadence"—decay—decline—a declining—cadēre—a fall.*

♎︎

Quarantine has disrupted our notion of home. Our
present conception of time has been deeply distorted. I
think that's why I keep thinking about Bruno K. Öijer's
poems. If and when things go back to normal, is a return
to familiarity really possible? The new normal might be
unheimlich for a while. Or, things might also never be
the same.

> *it's a lie that we've come home*
> *we'll never come home*
> *none of us will ever come home*
> (from *The Trilogy*, 202)

♎︎

It feels like we've been falling for a while now.
What year is this?
De-, our new de-fault mode.
We are sick.
What month is this?
We are sick.
Therefore, we make Art.
What day is this?
We don't know it, but we *are* Decadent again.

♎︎

When it comes to our ailing, carved up planet of cerium
mines and Bagger 288s, I find I have an increasingly inti-

mate understanding of my own mortality (a thanatopic intimacy). Lodged in the present, I feel like a Decadent in the same way many contemporary artists think of themselves as avant-garde. The 'avant-garde' is not necessarily a historically fixed phenomenon and I believe the same is true of Decadence. Ideologically, the Decadence of the arsenic-yellow 1890s feels reminiscent of the Graveyard Poets of the eighteenth century. And what about the Gothic? For instance, is Wilde's *Picture of Dorian Gray* a Decadent novel or a Gothic novel?

The Gothic is unmistakably an ancestor of Decadence.

When I read James Pate's *Flowers Among the Carrion: Essays on the Gothic in Contemporary Poetry*, I found myself thinking of vast, monstrous night as a hyperobject in the same way Timothy Morton has approached global climate change as a hyperobject. If night is a metaphor for the unknown in the Gothic, then I can understand why Gothicism keeps springing up in contemporary poetry. It feels like an appropriate response to the Anthropocene, to global climate change. Metaphorically, Decadence embraces night—inevitable death. But Decadence also feels like a warming. Warming like the earth itself. Burning up like Walter Pater's "gem-like flame" or Gustave Moreau's sublime painting of Salome: "[...] glowing coals, as violet as jets of gas, as blue as burning alcohol, as white as the rays of a star. The horrific head blazes, still bleeding, leaving clots of dark purple on the ends of the beard and hair" (*À rebours*).

The light or gem-like flame of Decadence is not the same thing as the contrasting "daylight" (optimistic, good-humoured U.S. poetry) Pate mentions in *Flowers Among the Carrion*. Decadence contains a fleeting, blood-stained light—fuelled by sickness and oppression, society's wars and violence. It is the last moments of light just before nightfall.

Whether I think of myself as a Graveyard Poet leaning into Night, a Gothicized Decadent, or a zombie-Romantic, there's a lot of influences at work in my poetry and I see all of those things as valuable to how I approach the Anthropocene.

So, when it comes to the state of American poetry, what might a New Decadence look like?

1. Will Alexander, Aase Berg, Daniel Borzutzky, Marty Cain, Feng Sun Chen, Don Mee Choi, CA Conrad, Olivia Cronk, LaTasha N. Nevada Diggs, Kate Durbin, Joshua Escobar, Shelley Fellers, t'ai freedom ford, Lara Glenum, Johannes Görannson, Duriel Harris, Christian Hawkey, Ana Hofmann, Valerie Hsiung, Kim Hyesoon, Dylan Krieger, Sade LaNay, Ji Yoon Lee, Dawn Lundy Martin, Madison McCartha, Joyelle McSweeney, Valerie Mejer-Caso, Vi Khi Nao, James Pate, Raquel Salas Rivera, Jake Skeets, Abraham Smith, Ed Steck, Jake Syersak, Cecilia Vicuña, Ronaldo Wilson, Candice Wuehle, Justin Wymer, Kim Yideum, Raúl Zurita and many others.

If a New Decadence exists in 2020, then it *must* include translations or interlingual works. For example, LaTasha N. Nevada Diggs' sonically mesmerizing *TwERK* incorporates over 12 different languages.

What could possibly be more threatening—contagious and corrupting, posing a danger to America's gold standards of poetry—than the threat of the foreign, the excess of translation?

2. New Decadents will use translation to combat ennui. Translation is linguistic drag. Use translation to hack into, inhabit the form of another. You will learn more about "you," than you ever thought possible. Not fluent in more than one language? Good news:

3. New Decadence powders its face in the datastream of the Internet. Google Translate is holy. Duolingo is holy. If you devote yourself to the cause, you can learn a new language in a matter of months. You can learn multiple languages in a matter of years.

"All writers must now be translators, and monolingual types will be regarded under suspicion of provincialism. Demographics and frontiers must be constantly fractured, and artistic concerns rotated into new contexts" ("Against Neo-Passéism").

Sway proudly, from language to language, you glowing chandelier!

4. New Decadence is maximalist in its scope.

5. New Decadence is not exclusively European. This is simply an impossibility because of translation. Such Decadence spreads like a beautiful virus. To this day, it is contagious. It is contagion itself. One need not look any further than Charles Baudelaire's own "transgressive circulation," his incredible journey (via translation) into Chinese (where he was referred to as a "demon poet" in the 1920s) and Russian (in what Adrian Wanner has described as Russia's 1880s pre-Decadence). Later Russian champions of Decadence would include N.M. Minsky, D.S. Merezhkovsky, and K.D. Balmont.

It is "in the very air" and it always has been.

6. New Decadence is whatever threatens the delicate sensibilities of the American canon.

7. New Decadence is Mondo Trasho, New Decadence is drunk with gossip! Gossip ensures the living become the undead.

8. New Decadence is mallrat flâneurie! New Decadence does not window-shop, but shoplifts from top fashion retailers and, as Justin Isis warns, "simplicity is the enemy of beauty."

9. New Decadence is about the truth of masks, queer camp, the contortion and crossing of languages, translation, performance, excess—and excess above all.

10. New Decadence is unapologetically Queer.

Queerness is the truest of crimes! A Queer is always-already gossip! Every time I translate foreign poems into English, my threat level rises! My bilingual poems, my Queer camp, my puns, my gore, my excess.

My poetry is my *weapon*.

Audre Lorde: "I am here because I am greedy, and curious. I believe I am an endangered species the same way each of you is endangered, and *poetry* is a weapon" (*Conversations with Audre Lorde*)

11. There is nothing sincere about Decadence. Which is why there is nothing more sincere than Decadence.

12. New Decadence is not about charity. Charity is the illusion of progress itself. Its effect is only temporary. Feeding the homeless isn't the same thing as *housing* the homeless. The "whole" of society is sick. The individual is "starved." Individualism, as Wilde argues, is "what through Socialism we are to attain."

13. New Decadence means the flowers of your poetry must possess "contortions of tendrils" and "unusual lacerations." Your flowers must be obscene, like the ones Bataille describes in "The Language of Flowers."

Curvy, fatty, swollen flowers—fat-lipped flowers.

"At any rate, it is a very queer new sort of quarterly." Critics were outraged by the Decadence of *The Yellow Book* and Aubrey Beardsley's illustrations were often dismissed as grotesque and pornographic. In a 1894 issue of *The National Observer*, an anonymous critic resorted to using medical terms to criticize the "hyper-sebaceous" and "fatty" Decadence of the third volume of *The Yellow Book*:

"The truth is that Mr. Beardsley scorns to picture any person who is not suffering from xanthelasma, which is defined in medical books as an appearance 'caused by hypertrophy of sebaceous glands and fatty degeneration of the subcutaneous connective tissue.' This extreme xanthelasma is the reason that Mr. Beardsley's figures are attenuated where you would expect plumpness, and sebaceous where you would expect them to be slim. Mr. Max Beerbohm's caricature of George IV. is also hyper-sebacious [...]"

Art that is "hyper-sebaceous" or "fatty"—*too much*—is always a threat to the "ordinariness" of the poetry establishment. Especially when it comes to American poetry.

Given Bataille's emphasis on hidden and dirty root systems, the etymology of the word "obscene" is important. Coming from the Latin (*obscēnus*), if something has been labelled *ob*-scene, this means one of society's many repressive state apparatuses has decided a particular image should be *ob*-structed from the view of spectators. The *ob*-scene is what's *not* seen.

The image of a field of flowers in a poem alone isn't Decadent simply because it is an image containing *many* flowers. There has to be *too many* of them. An obscene number. One must consider them a nuisance. A threat to Taste. Threateningly kitschy. *Too much.*

If the obscenity of flowers poses a threat to tasteful or overtly masculine art, then that is precisely what makes flowers a valuable tool for New Decadent art.

14. New Decadent femininity is always a threat to fascism.

15. New Decadence is more and more. In contemporary poetry, the word itself—"Decadence"—keeps springing up, flower-like. Olivia Cronk, in her new book *Womonster*, asks, "Did you ever get into the stagnant bath of a real confession? Slip inside into living in a body as a site of decadent filth?" In "Digital Fauna," Ginger Ko's speaker confesses, "I like the decadent privacy of text." At the same time, the poem can be read as a caution against ambivalence.

Citing the same aforementioned Joyelle McSweeney article in their introduction, *Quarterly West* launched a "Decadence"-themed issue in 2020. Amy Sailer's Introduction to the issue is a strange one because many of the so-called "Decadent" poems do not come across as "sick" or "corrupted," but some do make references to sickness. In fact, a number of the poems are arguably tidy, formatted in tightly woven tercets or couplets. That's not to say that the lyric can't be sonically excessive (look no further than *Toxicon & Arachne!*), but the Gothic also feels removed from (not all) but many of these poems. Some are arguably teetering on the cusp of minimalism. These "Decadent" poems do not feel transgressive, de-generative, or thermally degenerative. There is certainly nothing *obscene* here. (When someone says "Decadence," Carl Phillips might be the last poet I think of.) It feels more like an anthology of well-crafted, Impressionistic works with, at times, mild Rococo elements (i.e. a lot of the poems incorporate words like "gold" or "golden" etc). Judging by the Introduction, the obscene feels as though it has been swapped out for Arthur Symons' ideals...

"Now Impressionist and Symbolist have more in com-mon than either supposes; both are really working on the same hypothesis, applied in different directions. What both seek is not general truth merely, but *la vérité vraie*, the very essence of truth—the truth of appear-ances to the senses, of the visible world to the eyes that see it; and the truth of spiritual things to the spiritual vision" (Arthur Symons, "The Decadent Movement in Literature," 1893).

In the same essay, Symons cites Decadence as what's "in the very air." He seemed to want to *cure* the city cafes of a mysterious pollution. A cure for something that often has no traction in academic circles (i.e. *If we split up this 'disease' of Art into Impressionism and Symbolism, we can elevate the conversation, we can think we understand how this disease works*).

Impressionism and Symbolism are *appropriate* things to discuss in academia, not just because they supposedly reveal the "truth of the human soul," but because they are born from out of institutions. They have always been a way to explain Decadence. But Decadence and excess? Such things are ironically still taboo in blood-lacquered academia.

Again, while I wasn't necessarily disappointed with poems by contributors like Brian Clifton and Emily Pittinos, I feel like the New Decadence of our sick world calls for a "contortion" of languages.

16. New Decadence must demand high-risk poetry.

Poetries-in-translation.

17. James Pate: "In the Gothic, we are no longer placed on a pedestal above other phenomena due to History or God or Nature. In the Gothic, we are small beings under the night sky, limited in our knowing and capabilities. There is always a House of Usher or a planet called Melancholia to remind us of our finitude" (*Flowers Among the Carrion*)

Quarantine feels like haunted sleep. We think we wake up to the news and coffee each morning, but it's just more retweets of the same irrational nightmare.

The same sickness. It never goes away.

What day is this?

18. The future was never a continuation of the present.

The future only contaminates the present.

NATURE

Sailor Stephens

Neo-Decadence requires the ability to shape & direct reality. We cannot manifest magick without an adherence to occult practices. We cannot speak of the Occult without speaking of Nature.

A modern dandy would do well to draw energy from growth, decay, chaos. In the age of Instagram, Naturalism is dead. Pure artifice is the default.

In contrast to the drab mediocrity of Dollskill & "dad trainers" & YouTube makeup tutorials, modern Nature has a fresh aesthetic. Forget the dreary old woman of the past, the New Nature is all grand gestures & pathetic fallacy.

A dead rabbit in its furs & red jewels lying in a Tesco carpark. A ruined office block with trees exploding through the walls, heavy with rotting apples.

10 simple acts of nature-based Neo-Decadence;

1. Dress inappropriately for the outdoors & stumble around, tying ribbons around branches.

2. Wade through inner city wastelands, until your vintage suede boots are caked in mud.

3. Stuff the pockets of your bootcut PVC jeans with random foliage & insects.

4. Bury your clothes and let them rot before digging them up & wearing them clubbing.

5. Have your drag persona be a tree.

6. Dry piles & piles of flowers in your house until every room is a fire hazard.

7. Go moonbathe in archive McQueen then cast banishing rituals on your landlord.

8. Invite feral dogs into your garden.

9. Dance on the roof of a ruined mansion in the fog.

10. Go outside on a clear night & cover your lovely face with bugs.

AGAINST NEO-PASSEISM

Justin Isis
Damian Murphy
Gaurav Monga
Quentin S. Crisp
LC von Hessen

1. The Neo-Passéist type is a recognizable fixture of the current psychosocial landscape. There are, among others, meliorative Neo-Passéists, nihilist Neo-Passéists, spiritual Neo-Passéists and literary/artistic Neo-Passéists. All are creatures of glaring internal contradictions, and while contradictions are useful for producing interest when ground together intentionally (as this manifesto itself does, being the work of multiple authors with differing views), the unwitting Neo-Passéist is a mere vector or vehicle for ambient market forces and their associated manners, unaware of how ridiculous they appear. The absolutely sincere, guilty, anxious and agonized cast is characteristic of most current art.

2. Neo-Passéism is the unexamined artistic logic of capitalist realism.

3. The goal of the Neo-Passéist writer is to be a professional, and "professionalism" they take to imply "authenticity" (equally specious). The commercial Sublime validates their tedious notions of "hard work," "craftsmanship," networking, self-promotion and the like. With splendid irony, the American-style "individualist" market has produced a publishing industry maintained by a limited class and caste of writers, most of them educated at the same schools, occupying the same social position and aiming for contracts with the same small group of presses. Admittance to writing programs and workshops is seen as proof of "seriousness," when it is merely slavishness. No medieval guild could be more dispiriting or predictable in its transmission of cliches.

4. The Neo-Passéist is deeply and quite defensively concerned with *not* being perceived or defined as Neo-Passéist.

5. Nothing makes the Neo-Passéist happier than the translation or sublimation of a literary work into another medium. Short stories (particularly compelling or topical examples of which are offhandedly referred to as "articles") are seen as kernels for films, while novels should now inspire streaming television series, and both are praised for the extent to which they function as disguised journalism or self-help. The Neo-Passéist, uncomfortable with literature, longs for it to be anything other than itself, tolerating it to the extent that it ignores all modern technical and stylistic developments since the 19th century advent of Symbolism.

6. For the Neo-Passéist, literature and art are civic projects intended to reinforce the prejudices of a subcultural elite, reassuring them that they are "good people" with the appropriate slants, guilts and sympathies. This includes a reflexive disdain for "wasting time"; consequently the average Neo-Passéist will not engage with a given work unless some perceived virtue is appended through crudely applicable life lessons, "uplifting" themes, displays of performative wokeness, or stores of easily-digested cultural capital in the form of studiously researched depictions of the "experiences" of a particular group (reinforcing the hub-and-spokes, monocultural model of art—the opposite of true crosscultural collaboration).

7. The Neo-Passéist's concealed, puritan disgust for language implies a prophylactic approach to writing; words must be kept at arm's length, not given too much importance. The literary Neo-Passéist, despite their professed debt to the written works of the past, feels more at home with the reassuring cleanliness of moving images and their controlled tempos. The internal construction capabilities of language are seen as suggestive, treacherous, gratuitous: ever present is the fear that language might escape from its subordinate position of "representing" a recognizable social field, or be used by well-versed adepts to fracture reality itself. Neo-Passéists are terrified to admit that language exists in the same way their physical bodies exist: this fear prevents them from being poets, or feeling deeply beyond a thin scum of anxiety and its corresponding need for validation. But for the Neo-

Decadent poet, language, produced inside the body like a spider's gleaming strands, forms both their weapon and their home.

8. Neo-Passéism can be summarized by the phrase "reality hunger."

9. Capitalism, having appropriated all available physical markets, has moved on to conquering time. Its success can be measured by the extent to which we are trapped in numerous overlapping "era markets" running on commodified nostalgia. The cycle has accelerated, so that while a fallow period of ten to twenty years once preceded each sequence of revivals and remakes, the profitable gravity is now irresistible, and the 1980s—dragged back from the dead at the start of the millennium—show no sign of ending. This "capitalist time hole" has produced an eternal present, with no possibility of escape from its event horizon. Hauntology remains only a shadowy awareness of cancelled futures, and the deterioration of art results as "creatives" are expected to engage with recognizable "content" to expand vast corporate franchises. The production mechanics of this "intellectual property" then become the governing principles of creation. The emotions of Neo-Passéists overflow into these tired vessels, and the final result is a sort of constipated myth cycle, the promise of various dithering apocalypses that never fully arrive. With this new feudalism of film franchises, fiction series from corporate publishing houses, and repetitive gallery shows displaying the artists of the past (all of it presided over by the academic guilds), we have reached an entirely medieval age.

10. 21st century literary movements have thus far produced nothing of any interest. The fault lies not with a perceived cultural turn away from writing, or any other cliched idea of decline, but with the inferior personalities and "talents" of those involved with the likes of alt-lit, Bizarro, etc; to put it plainly, all 21st century literary movements until now have been Neo-Passéist. Most of them consist of an easily replicable series of stylistic tics, usually grouped around a few intermittently charismatic figures who are incessantly copied by thoughtless sycophants, to ever diminishing returns. Meanwhile, outmoded journals, newspapers, magazines and other legacy organs perpetuate the worship of the dead, while professors foist their third-rate thoughts on the young, all but entombing them before they can write. But literature is neither a guild system nor a subculture.

Tomorrow and today
we're tired of quiet
cat-coddling
introspective
bespectacled
unspectacular
impostors with syndromes:
aging emerging artists
abiding in guilty and/
or "compassionate" lassitude
for fear of intimately dismantling
or even just brassily violating
the most profitably stable, anxious and

sustainable
tribal
life-lies.

11. The Neo-Passéist commits the basic error of con-flating emotions produced by artworks encountered in childhood with the underlying value of these artworks. The result is a flattening of historical complexities, a Disneyfication of the past, a continuous and numbing revival of old kitsch. We are sold the lesser so that we will forget the greater. Eliade has already pointed out that *homo religiosus* is afflicted with a nostalgia for reality, for that time when reality was most intense, the time of Creation, in *illo tempore*. *Sehnsucht* is the beginning of this greater nostalgia. Once, we are told, Diogenes the Cynic stood outside a brothel and shouted, "A beautiful whore is like poisoned honey." The Neo-Passéist, unable to tell which honey is poisoned and which not, passes all honey by.

12. Genres have replaced proper stylistic movements. This has resulted in endless tedium; therefore we proclaim market-driven, intentional genre writing to be another symptom of Neo-Passéism. The inherent value of genre, once subversive, has become its own orthodoxy. Against it stands the clerical call for "high art" and a return to "Tradition". Both these positions are untenable, and so the blasphemy of disdaining genre must be committed, while at the same time the pompous reactionary esteem for liberal humanist social novels and the like must be deflated like a gaseous balloon. We will simply ransack

everyday life as it pleases us!!! There is nothing to be said about "the human" that is not readily apparent to a child. At the same time we are BORED with all genres, corporate spectacles, straitjackets of profitable rules (the mere recombination of tropes does not constitute innovation or interest). Away with the tedium of crime, horror, fantasy and the rest. Away, too, with "transgression"—the tamest and most predictable of them all. To avoid stagnation, we will ensure that all of our tropes cancel themselves out. We will combine tawdry eroticism with statistical anecdotes, and antinatalist parables with romantic Young Adult adventures. We will exalt violently diverse artistic personalities, Post-Naturalist prose styles, "bad writing" whenever necessary. Pieties and epiphanies will be ridiculed and cancelled. While the Neo-Passéist uses genre as camouflage to conceal their own ideological and imaginative bankruptcy, the Neo-Decadent removes its earmarks altogether until nothing remains but the aftertaste. The reader, nonetheless, will be convinced they are reading genre fiction, though it will be impossible to pinpoint what makes it so. In this way, genre can be liberated from itself, leaving the artist free to clothe their inspiration in the spirit that remains.

13. Under Neo-Passéism, fictional works are routinely conceived as transcriptions of mental movies: an orthodoxy as bland as the three decker novel of the 19th century. Television and film (almost always denoting filmed theatre, rather than video art as such) are not to be taken as the apotheosis of art, any more than undue credence should be given to Pater's misguided notion about all

art aspiring to the condition of music: we might just as easily imagine all music aspiring to the condition of sculpture, or all video games aspiring to the condition of poetry (these would be more productive avenues for exploration, were they to be pursued seriously). While advances such as the *nouveau roman* updated fiction, they brought their own set of limitations, principally a dependence on visual surfaces. We, the Neo-Decadents, will restore a focus on taste, smell, touch, and inner realms of sensation that until now have been only clumsily apprehended by the languages of neuroscience and psychology. Fully equipped with esoteric faculties and their ability to penetrate beyond the visual, we will produce psychic and spiritual cross sections far outstripping the crude automatism of the Surrealists and the blunt mechanical cut-ups of the past century. The expansion of sensory detail—sensory experience—thus forms one of our prime objectives. Wearying transcriptions of social customs, marriage plots and the like can only be regarded as irrelevant strictures for the tired and unambitious. Against the Neo-Passéist school of would-be directors and showrunners, we put forward abrupt works hewing to no trite structures, no story arcs, collapsing distinctions between internal and external realities, under no obligation to resolve or explain anything. Neglected filmic techniques of juxtaposition and altered perspective may be employed when necessary, but always with a focus on literary texture.

14. The Neo-Passéist makes themselves central by making themselves invisible. They hide behind the camera.

When an actor resembling the hidden Neo-Passéist appears in front of the camera, they call the result 'relatable'. Relatable to what? For a moment, let a drone with a faulty circuit carry the camera. Now all kinds of things appear in the field of view, all kinds of candidates for mutual relations: seagulls and petrol stations, for instance, or kebabs and midwives. Now, in order to talk of 'relating', we must say what relates to what.

15. Neo-Decadence, by its very nature, subverts all attempts at appropriation. To wield it for sociopolitical ends is like grasping the tip of a blade. Any blood spilled in such foolishness only sharpens its edge and makes it all the more treacherous. The Neo-Passéist, being as tenacious as they are banal, will thus injure themselves again and again while the Neo-Decadent artist has already moved on to new forms of expression.

16. Art emerges from the intersection of theft, deception, vandalism and parody. Therefore we exalt all lies and hoaxes, deliberate frauds, appropriations, and other such schemes to deceive the gullible. Our natural faculties have been bound for too long by the anaemic tyranny of the simple and sincere. Life is fantastically deceitful and complex. Any art that is not at least equally so is a faulty mirror.

17. Posterity is a form of speculation involving artistic capital. We advise against investing in posterity, given the inevitable persistence of Neo-Passéism. It is better to deliberately go artistically bankrupt in real time: ideas do not exist to be hoarded.

18. Style is not and can never be "a pane of glass." Linguistic associations constitute their own reality, not separate from or subordinate to other subjective experiences of everyday life: our lives are inside novels and poems as much as novels and poems are objects in our lives. "Honest" use of language is always and only ever propaganda. We exalt the sticky, gummy, opaque, constructive and viral character of words. The creative repurposing and misuse of fashionable neologisms will provide no shortage of entertainment. Purists and pre-scriptivists are of no importance, capable as they are only of shallow reactions.

19. The Neo-Decadent writer sees no reason to regard their prose as anything less than a vehicle of prophecy. Plato, in the Phaedrus, identifies four types of benevolent madness: the oracular madness of Apollo, the feverish and holy delirium inspired by Dionysus, the poetic madness of the muses, and the philosophic madness of the love-struck savant. When combined, these comprise an invisible grammar of inordinate flexibility, having the power to provoke fits of insubordination in the unsuspecting reader. This can be used to give rise to insurgency in the halls of academia, to incite what amounts to peasant revolts among genre presses and fiction conventions, and to stir discontent in the hearts of readers who would otherwise settle for the most market-driven works of art. The texts that inspire these outbursts will remain entirely unsuspected. On the surface, they will appear to be unremarkable, if original and somewhat outré.

20. Autobiography and memoir: the purest fraudulence. Solipsists of the "authentic" must not be invited to parties.

Until each analytic entitled
pestilential essayist chokes
audibly,

we cancel our attention and
drag the future away from us
intimately:

saints' unspooling innards;
language is still our plastic inner
anatomy.

21. Sentimentality and convention are both ugly and marketable. Neo-Decadence, conversely interested in beauty of the strictest sort, will at first appear revolting, tedious, absurd, inconclusive, uncategorizable. This is not a paradox: our work will appear ugly to the ugly, beautiful to the beautiful (mere surfaces have nothing to do with it).

22. Canned myths and folkloric fakery, if used in art and writing, should at least not be taken seriously. "Updating" cliches of this kind in the light of currently fashionable values is a low level trick.

23. Music should not be substituted for identity. There is no designated Neo-Decadent musical style, but too many Neo-Passéist ones to count.

24. The immense freedom permitted by the Internet and other advancing technologies calls for a truly cross-cultural, altermodern artistic movement. Not limiting ourselves to English, we will establish Spanish, Japanese, Urdu, Arabic, Chinese, Russian, and other Neo-Decadent literatures. All writers must now be translators, and monolingual types will be regarded under suspicion of provincialism. Demographics and frontiers must be constantly fractured, and artistic concerns rotated into new contexts.

25. To relieve boredom, Neo-Decadent factions will be established on every continent and, ideally, in every country, always with the aim of undermining the pompous, tendentious, sincere, academic, intellectual, stultifying, risible and outdated impersonators of writers and artists who in most cases comprise the publishing industries and art scenes. Fashion, music, writing, art, cooking, sexuality and all other areas of everyday life will be dismantled and reformulated whenever boredom threatens to constrain us.

26. When Li Tang painted *Wind in Pines Among the Myriad Valleys*, it was the wind he was painting, though it was the pines and valleys that were visible. This is not simply to say that he had mastered a technique for showing movement in a still picture. The wind, here, has

another meaning. The art is in the artist, and this is what is passed on—what is most secret and most alive. The artwork is merely the visible remains of the art. Those who have first understood the wind in the pines will understand the artwork. The Neo-Passéist will simply think it is a picture of pines.

27. A reader or a viewer of art stands at once inside and outside a world. For the Neo-Passéist materialist there can never be an outside; in this metaphysical colour-blindness they are disqualified from engagement with art. The naive materialists, those seeking reality of any kind in the world of "identities," "meaningful experience" and the like will certainly never find it. Failing to discover themselves, they will produce only increasingly monotonous period pieces. The attempt to reproduce experience exactly as it is leads only to a flavourless distortion of the real. In order to express something genuine, one must be willing to wander without aim or discretion, to go blindfolded into a minefield, and to submit to processes that cannot be understood in terms of any existing model.

28. The Neo-Passéist materialist is like a colonial Victorian gentleman. Just as such a gentleman could not conceive that another culture might be anything but "mumbo jumbo" (a term first applied by the colonisers to an idol reportedly worshipped in Africa), so the Neo-Passéist, a missionary bent on improving the universe after his own design, cannot conceive that the universe might have designs of its own. Even now, in supposedly cutting-edge philosophical circles, the word "spooky" is

so prevalent as to have entered into the argot of the field. It is assumed that any challenge to materialism is, to swap words for the same effect, mumbo jumbo. The subtext is clear: the universe would be dashed impudent to disobey whatever rules the Neo-Passéist arrives at with the empirical method (which, itself, can never be empirically validated). The philosopher J.J.C. Smart, pioneer of the materialist theory that the mind is the brain, stating first that the mind must obey the laws of physics like everything else, said that the idea of *psychophysical laws* has "a queer smell". From this point of view, the Neo-Decadent artist is certainly among those who are *reality-queer*.

29. Easy spiritual binaries of "theistic" and "nontheistic" approaches do little to challenge the unquestioned materialist framework of Neo-Passéist ontology. Neo-Decadent occultism, operating outside these categories, represents a flexible, animistic, non-transcendental yet non-materialist framework for hijacking social and psychic reality fields: this is Post-Naturalism. Neo-Passéist occultism, in contrast, has long since exhausted its methods, and comprises little more than an inversion of New Atheism, ignorant of both the unfathomable ocean of tradition and anti-tradition and the untapped potential that lies before us. The Neo-Decadent, looking back on thousands of years of praxis, from the necromantic funerary rites of the ancient Greeks to the extravagant practices of Mao Shan Taoists, sees a thousand million reliquaries, an unending chain of treasure houses, some well-guarded and others unattended, and a banquet that could not be exhausted by all the gluttons in the world.

The Neo-Passéist sees little more than a few over-utilized horror tropes and a sneaking suspicion that God is a bastard.

30. Our current crop of nihilists are at least as attenuated as their forebears, but they lack even the redeeming Romantic grandeur. They are as guilty as any Christian, as preening as any liberal moralist and as inhibited as any repressed virgin. The nihilist/pessimist Neo-Passéist will, for example, proclaim the need to end the human race to "save the planet," not realizing the extent of their own ego projection. Distanced and divorced from the universe, they deny their affinity with empty space while exalting themselves in a self-enclosed bubble. This clot of mentation they alternately dread and worship. These mechanists, tedious as any Redemptionist, haunted by the demon of consciousness, are hopelessly incapable of art. Neo-Decadence, arising from garbage heaps of tragic absurdity, refuses the easy lure of tragedy.

Are these anaemic priests
the prophesied Dionysian beasts?

Somewhere in isolated rewriting
is the sense of the unfiltered
nationless aristocrat
of poverty
scaling beyond
"relatability."

Thieves of the Absolute
and nomadic vandals of
irrelevant everyday
beautiful forfeiture.

31. The Neo-Passéist views "romantic love" in terms of clichéd visual and audio shorthand rather than surplus emotion, and likewise views ensuing relationships in terms of status symbols and obligatory commodities to obtain through simplistic if/then logic ("*If* I want to fully qualify as an adult, *then* I must marry and reproduce," etc.). The Neo-Passéist Woman views the acquisition of a husband as the most important and life-affirming decision she will ever make, acquiring likewise a theoretical purpose and identity, while the Neo-Passéist Man views the acquisition of a wife in the sense that he might, upon achieving a promotion at work, acquire a newer model of car with which to impress his neighbours and business associates; the society they comprise views this disparity as quite natural and unworthy of comment. The Neo-Decadents, eschewing both cynicism and earnestness, follow Rimbaud's dictum that "love must be reinvented" on individual terms.

32. Romance in the fiction of the Neo-Passéist follows the unquestioning tradition of the original passéists in its depiction as obligatory, inevitable, and inherently positive, unless one party involved is portrayed in a clear and obvious manner as the villain in order to impart a ham-fisted moral lesson. It is typically a flabby appendage to the greater body of the work and bears little to no

resemblance to either a true connection or misconnection arising from the real world or the greatest heights and depths of florid fantasy—a hollow, fragile construction unable to survive beyond the book's end pages or the film's credits. The Neo-Passéist excuse for emotion is essentially propaganda for the most banal strain of pair-bonding, with conception and childrearing anticipated as the mandatory end result.

33. For the Neo-Passéist, poetry is either teenage effusion or empty elliptical gesture; everywhere grotesque cliche sits alongside bloated academic irrelevance. This situation amuses the Neo-Decadents greatly. In response, the image of the tortured guilt-ridden poet will be cleansed from the writer's consciousness. Self-loathing and self-promotion are two sides to a single coin, a currency so devoid of value as to pose a threat to the economy of culture. The inspired artist simply emits with as little self-consciousness as a flaming matchead, confident that an inferno will inevitably result, but unconcerned as to the details and disinclined to over-examine their work.

34. We extol a total merger of fiction and poetry, to whatever narrative ends we deem appropriate, beyond the tepid reach of "prose poems" and other predictable curios. Stories and novels may be told alternately in verse, in the form of lists, with contradictory narratives, in first and second and third person in sequence. Sampling and rephrasing of earlier works should be carried out whenever necessary, alongside the plundering of material from online sources and the exploration of possibilities inher-

ent in unconventional typography. Note, though, that these techniques are of no interest in and of themselves; there is nothing more risible than studious copyists reverently repeating the "experiments" of fifty or a hundred years before. Formal experimentation unmoored from true Neo-Decadent sensibility is as barren as conventional realism.

35. We must adopt the subversion of punctuation as an affront to commercial success. The likes of Christine Brooke-Rose, Arno Schmidt, and Maurice Roche have set the stage for a far more dangerous application of the footsoldiers of grammar. Imagine an entire novel composed of endless variations on the mis-use of the Oxford comma. The difficulty of the prospect only fans the flames of our enthusiasm. The first competent author to pull it off will be hailed among us as a literary hero. That their work is unpublishable will make it all the more essential.

36. Controlled, slow-paced narratives involving excessive use of the first-person singular often result in boredom. We follow the 'I' much too blindly and get bored much too soon. Narrative trajectories should continue to surprise the writer even whilst writing it and often overtake the writer, as a spring wound tightly suddenly releases. Of course, there is no good reason to remain consistent in regard to the narrator. The 'I' of the narrative might refer to several different entities throughout the course of a story, depending on context and indicated by subtle textual cues. Where it may appear that a single voice

unwinds the narrative thread, the discerning reader will detect a multiplicity of speakers, each impersonating the others as befits their own personal agenda. It is well known that the reader unconsciously identifies with the first-person voice no matter how much they might resist doing so. Where the narrator is akin to a prism, or to the shifting planes of a kaleidoscope, the reader is afforded the unique opportunity to confront the multitude within themselves.

37. The Victorian moralist critic has much in common with the Neo-Passéist Internet commentator, and we anticipate the future development of ever more earnest, guilty, principled, self-doubting, introspective, inelegant impostors who will call themselves writers, critics and artists. There is no assurance that any alterhuman trends will eliminate the Neo-Passéist tendency, regardless of what currently nonexistent media expressions they choose to manifest, in the same way that, when examining the output of literary critics in the 21st century, it is impossible not to be reminded of the shallow faceless gaping of jellylike creatures mindlessly drifting in oceanic darkness, or surly, flea-bitten hominids inspecting their leaky shelters and thinking them the most exalted palaces. Anticipating the atavistic resurgence of retrograde aesthetics, we pre-emptively mock the Future-Passéists of the 22nd and later centuries. Neither should potential synthetic intelligences be considered exempt from the reach of Neo-Passéism. Already we are inundated with clumsy, sentimental, reliable machines, and there is no reason to think the trend will expire.

38. Potential synthetic intelligences, writing machines and software should be hijacked and "misused" the moment they come into existence.

39. Uncritical stylistic adherence to any existing subculture should be regarded as a sign of laziness; Neo-Decadence cannot be fitted within the confines of punk, goth, dandyism or any current scene, including Internet-based image boards and fora. Writers, artists and clothing designers must be held to higher standards, while the slovenly and unimaginatively-dressed must be mocked. Although age is not necessarily an indicator of Neo-Passéist tendencies, in practice many older types are most likely beyond help at this point—but younger sorts should be encouraged to take their clothes as seriously as their prose. This will, to a great extent, revive the image of the poet-novelist and poet-designer as the forefront of the urban milieu.

40. Though not prizing commodified youth for its own sake, we are more interested in the productions of upcoming generations than in currying favour with those currently respected—who, for the most part, have created and tolerated the conditions that provoked this manifesto. It would be a trite exaggeration to say that anyone over thirty is irretrievably entrenched in a Neo-Passéist view of art, writing and fashion, but older writers and artists should not be uncritically regarded as deserving respect simply because they are well-known or have continued to produce material. On the other hand,

young creators should be held to high standards and not unjustly celebrated for producing mediocre work (or any work at all). Academia has grotesquely extended the apprentice phase: teenagers are already old enough to begin determining their artistic direction and pursuing it seriously (impostor syndrome is for impostors). Neo-Decadence as we conceive it will unfold over the course of the 21st century, and many of its most important practitioners are just now being born.

Deprived of time
from before birth;
deprived of an age
from after death?

The audience, thoughtfully, expires
from its anguished
pseudo-self-
regard. Unread,

the banquet begins;
dandelion flowers
of the electric
cemetery.

41. Given that Neo-Passéist tendencies are likely to continue into the future, we do not advocate a linear view of aesthetic time, but conceive of it as transpiring in various loops and spirals, flipping between past, present and future. Passéism, Neo-Passéism and the inevitable Future-Passéism also exist in dialogue with each other,

and it would not be inaccurate to speak of future trends retroactively influencing the current phase of existence. For example, we can say with reasonable accuracy that the most publicly applauded fictional work of 2120 will be a worthless period piece. Situated in 2020, we pre-emptively mock its "timeliness;" its "relevance" and "resonance" with its audience. The short-sighted present, used to reviewing only the past, must look forward to the oncoming tide of mediocrity and limitation. It is essential to review the future before it occurs.

42. We reserve a special curse for all Future-Passéist biographers, reviewers and critics of our work, and we task our own artistic descendants with reviewing the reviewers, criticizing the critics. Anyone speaking ill of the morals, life choices, and clothing styles of the Neo-Decadents should be patronized for their obvious Neo-Passéism. Future-Decadents situated even further along the spiral of aesthetic time will dispute the slander that we "haven't aged well" or are "products of our era" (when, in fact, we are consciously producing the time that cocoons us). Like pharaohs we are already embalming everything of ourselves that needs to be preserved, and from the proper perspective are aging better than any of our critics—many of whom, from our current point of view, do not yet exist. We will use outrageous fabrications and autobiographical inventions to confuse and disorient the pious scolds of the future who hope to reconstruct us with their sanctimonious ideological forensics. To our descendants with similar temperaments we leave the

entirety of our gilded and glittering artistic corpses. Our relics will be colourful trinkets used to produce whatever effects they find amusing and illuminating for their own experiments.

43. Drug use, promiscuous sex, a nomadic lifestyle and excessive indulgence in retro gaming are basic elements of everyday existence, not exaggerated markers of personal expansion or artistic challenge. One might as well describe the violently ecstatic taste of a cheese sandwich. While the Neo-Passéist addresses the reader exactly as they are, the Neo-Decadent writes to what they might become given sufficient effort. This effort is encouraged by the writing itself, which is carefully contrived to wage a continual assault upon its audience. This is not done by insulting them or by attempting to shock or disgust, but through subtle acts of deception that, if successful, pass unnoticed.

44. Suicides are to be afforded neither special esteem nor exaggerated sympathy. Others will take their place. At the same time, we don't begrudge those wishing to depart the Neo-Passéist social field.

45. Be wary of those too eager for commercial success and those constantly seeking to dine out on what in reality may be very modest achievements. Many of the most well-regarded and comprehensively networked types are utter mediocrities. While exposure is the guiding grail of the Neo-Passéist, the Neo-Decadent seeks isolation as a

matter of virtue. Neo-Decadent factions prefer to remain as marginalized as possible. True worth has a natural tendency to keep itself concealed. The most exquisite art is not only hidden, but fiercely guarded.

46. The art forms that escape the spectacle are the ones that are so marginalized as to be considered negligible. Swiftly moving targets are much harder to pin down and commodify. Art should be duplicitous, concealing its true content beneath layers of subtext that will remain untouched even if it is colonized, absorbed or recuperated. There are types of expression and experience that can only be reached through arduous work, which, ironically, is the one thing a Neo-Passéist audience will never consent to under any circumstances. The nature of the spectacle is such that it must be served up on a platter.

47. Interior design should include an element of one's psyche splayed out on the walls: hence maximalism is preferable to a bland aping of the absurdly rich who can afford to "master-cleanse" the contents of their own skulls. The glistening skyscraper is a hypodermic needle injecting an aesthetic soporific into the heart of the urban populace. Allegedly extraneous architectural flourishes meant purely for the pleasure of the eye must return to standard form. Minimalism is like a hideous tax accountant with a protruding jaw who has not even the good sense to wear clashing colours.

48. Genuine innovation should not be confused with the generically shiny and new meant to distract children

and consumers. Nor should novelty in itself constitute superiority: a belief no less reactionary than that of those who would prefer culture and its morés to remain strictly fixed in time like the ruins of Pompeii. The Neo-Decadents blast all technologies into the future in a tiger's leap; we are, however, not well-kempt technocrats working at hipster cafes. We like things raw, often perhaps even filthy, for we revel in the possibility of the real destruction and open ruin of all old city streets that need to be repaved every year with cobblestones and pocked with cathedrals that were bombed and rebuilt to make them look as if they were not only tombs of the living.

49. The Neo-Decadents exist at the intersection of multiple registers, a heteroglossia of images, words, clothes, facial expressions, fashion choices and manners. Apart from being outrageous—as if we were always either entering or exiting a carnival—we prize humour as essential to life and encourage jokes that are perverse, bold and unsympathetic; and as we think and write in different languages, it would not be unheard of for an absurdly comic Punjabi joke to be couched in a story written in English, producing discordant novelty, for one must first have to build in order to have an appetite to destroy, not so dissimilar to surgeons who desire meat after having spent an entire day gazing at viscera and repairing ruptured organs.

50. In the marketplace, stalls stand either side of a broad street crowded with people. Behind the stalls, leading away from the market, are numerous narrow and dingy

alleys. There is little or nothing to advertise what can be found down these turnings-off and most people stay on the main thoroughfare, confident that anything of worth has been laid before them on the visible stalls. Others have done the work of sifting and only the best quality goods make it to this street where the cost of space is so high. Life is short, too. There is neither time nor incentive to enter the side-alleys. Others, however, have gone past the stalls and entered the narrow passages running betweens buildings. They have explored, become lost, died in strange circumstances. Some return, however, to the marketplace at intervals, their clothes, speech, manner, their very faces changed. They have become different from those who browse the stalls and different from each other. Those who have never left the main street do not understand them. They look at them askance. As for those who have delved, perhaps one entered the alley of incense-makers, deeper and deeper, and found a temple under whose shadowy roof the incense of other times and places mixed; another entered the alley of carpet and tapestry makers, deeper and deeper, and spent years in contemplation of a tapestry woven in a stellate pattern of multi-lateral symmetry; another entered the alley of horologes, deeper and deeper, and lived by the time of different devices, with different rhythms of day and night in a different calendar. And so on. When they see each other again in the marketplace, even in their differences they recognise something they have in common. They have delved, and talk to each other of what they have found. The others wonder how they talk to each other when each now seems to speak a different language. They, the ones who stayed in the broad street, all speak the same language, and yet, when they are resting with others of their kind, they are sometimes discomfited by the sensation that there is nothing to say in this language. They resort to boasting of what they bought in the market. When it is time to die, they are troubled by the thought that they missed something, or have forgotten something important. But how could that be? They lived at the very centre of the world. Their names will be passed on, furnishing the minds of future generations like the goods displayed on the market stalls.

Too much toast
and all of the fried tomatoes—
the consumer of an unbalanced breakfast
rises early enough
for it to still seem late.

A PARTIAL LIST OF SNUGGLY BOOKS

G. ALBERT AURIER *Elsewhere and Other Stories*
CHARLES BARBARA *My Lunatic Asylum*
S. HENRY BERTHOUD *Misanthropic Tales*
LÉON BLOY *The Desperate Man*
LÉON BLOY *The Tarantulas' Parlor and Other Unkind Tales*
ÉLÉMIR BOURGES *The Twilight of the Gods*
CYRIEL BUYSSE *The Aunts*
JAMES CHAMPAGNE *Harlem Smoke*
FÉLICIEN CHAMPSAUR *The Latin Orgy*
FÉLICIEN CHAMPSAUR
    The Emerald Princess and Other Decadent Fantasies
BRENDAN CONNELL *Unofficial History of Pi Wei*
BRENDAN CONNELL *The Metapheromenoi*
RAFAELA CONTRERAS *The Turquoise Ring and Other Stories*
ADOLFO COUVE *When I Think of My Missing Head*
QUENTIN S. CRISP *Aiaigasa*
LADY DILKE *The Outcast Spirit and Other Stories*
CATHERINE DOUSTEYSSIER-KHOZE *The Beauty of the Death Cap*
ÉDOUARD DUJARDIN *Hauntings*
BERIT ELLINGSEN *Now We Can See the Moon*
ERCKMANN-CHATRIAN *A Malediction*
ALPHONSE ESQUIROS *The Enchanted Castle*
ENRIQUE GÓMEZ CARRILLO *Sentimental Stories*
EDMOND AND JULES DE GONCOURT *Manette Salomon*
REMY DE GOURMONT *From a Faraway Land*
REMY DE GOURMONT *Morose Vignettes*
GUIDO GOZZANO *Alcina and Other Stories*
GUSTAVE GUICHES *The Modesty of Sodom*
EDWARD HERON-ALLEN *The Complete Shorter Fiction*
EDWARD HERON-ALLEN *Three Ghost-Written Novels*
RHYS HUGHES *Cloud Farming in Wales*
J.-K. HUYSMANS *The Crowds of Lourdes*
J.-K. HUYSMANS *Knapsacks*
COLIN INSOLE *Valerie and Other Stories*
JUSTIN ISIS *Pleasant Tales II*

.